Regis College Library
15 ST. MARY STREET
TORONTO, ONTARIO, CANADA
M4Y 2R5

A Canadian Bishop's Memoirs

Alex
CARTER:

A Canadian Bishop's
MEMOIRS

by Alex Carter

© Alexander Carter 1994

All proceeds from the sale of this book will go towards the Bishop Alexander Carter Charitable Fund.

Distributed by:
> Tomiko Publications
> P.O. Box 502
> North Bay, Ontario, P1B 8J1

Canadian Cataloguing In Publications Data

Carter, W.A. (Alexander W.)
  Alex Carter: a Canadian bishop's memoirs

ISBN 0-9692787-5-6

1. Carter, W.A. (Alexander W.). 2. Catholic Church - Bishops - Biography. 3. Bishops - Ontario - Sault Ste. Marie - Biography.
I. Title.

BX4705. C3A3 1994   282'.092   C93-093069-X

Cover Photographer: Ashley and Crippen Photographers, Toronto, Ontario. Used with permission.

All other photographs taken from the Bishop Alexander Carter Photographic Collection, Diocesan Archives, Diocese of Sault Ste. Marie. Used with permission.

Tom Harpur, "Celibacy still dogs Rome 20 years after heroic speech" in The Toronto Star, Sunday, October 6, 1991. Used with permission.

*Lovingly dedicated
to the memory of my parents
Tom and Mary Carter*

*and to all those with whom
I have journeyed over the course of
my life.*

CONTENTS

My Formative Years	1
Journey to the Priesthood	13
New Horizons	37
Experiences of a Young Priest	67
Challenged!	95
Called to be Bishop	127
The Second Vatican Council	163
The Post-Conciliar Years	193
Living the Vision	231
Chronology	248

ACKNOWLEDGEMENTS

I wish to express my sincere gratitude to my fellow Bishops, friends and co-workers, without whose encouragement the writing of this collection of memories would never have been accomplished.

to my niece Michele Carter, Betty Szilva and Bishop Bernard Pappin for their care in editing the original text;

to Father Jacques Monet, S.J., from the University of Sudbury, and his assistants Jeanie Lacroix and Debbie Sauvé for the time and effort devoted to researching the material;

to Father Greg Humbert, archivist of the Diocese of Sault Ste. Marie, for his keen interest and invaluable suggestions;

to Francis Donnelly for his advice and counsel;

to those other valued friends who contributed to the development and clarification of the manuscript in various ways;

and to Ted Szilva, who coordinated the work of editing, printing and publishing these Memoirs, my thanks and blessing.

FOREWORD

In writing the following pages, I am responding to requests which I have received from many of my fellow Bishops and from other friends and co-workers. I do not labour under any illusion concerning the small role I chanced to play in the Church and in the world during my more than three-quarters of a century. I do hope, however, that the task of recalling my experiences may help in some small way to contribute to the growing volume of works that deal with the life and tradition of the Catholic Church in our country and the response to Vatican II throughout the world.

In these pages I allow facts to speak for themselves. My intention is to recall some memories of events during my life and the various situations in which I found myself. For some, these reflections may provide new insights into the events that have taken place in the more than fifty years that I have been ordained a priest.

One's background has much to do with the way one tries to shape one's life. So, at the risk of being tiresome, I am going to begin with my earliest memories and just let things develop from there. Perhaps some of the early events in my life, the background from which I came, the people with whom I came into contact in those early years, may shed some light on experiences which came in later life - experiences which were very often exciting and challenging. Some had a real effect - not through me, but by the very nature of the events - on the development of the Church, and our understanding of Church.

I do not believe that I have the gift to express adequately my immense gratitude to the many people who have enriched my life - those who have shared with me the moments of joy and comforted me in times of trial and sorrow. Some of these were life-long friends; others joined me along the way. All helped me to live more fully the "human comedy" and the Divine Presence. God bless you all!

+Alex Carter

My Formative Years

As I look back over my eighty-five years, I am convinced that my experiences as a young boy growing up in Montreal profoundly influenced the course of my life. I was born of Irish Catholic parents and baptized in St. Michael's Parish in the north end of the city. A few years later, my parents, Tom and Mary Carter, moved the family to St. Patrick's Parish and it was there that my younger brother Emmett and I began our formal education.

Our family background was quite simple. When I was first named a bishop, a company offered to research our genealogy. It was discovered that my grandfather Carter's family came to Canada from Ireland in the 1840's. They settled in Quebec City and it was there that my father was born and raised. As a young man Dad travelled to New York to take a course in printing to prepare himself for a career in the newspaper business.

My mother's family, the Kerrs, lived in Upper Town Quebec City. They were also of Irish descent but they were rather upper-middle-class and apparently considered themselves to be fairly influential. When a young typesetter from the *Montreal Star* began to court her daughter, I understand that Grandmother Kerr was not too happy about the relationship. Fortunately for us, when Grandfather Kerr met my dad, he was quite impressed with him. He informed his rather dominating wife that he had found Tom Carter to be a very fine man and there was no reason at all for discouraging Mary, or "Minnie" as they called her, from keeping company with him. Thus began our Carter family.

My mother was a very religious woman and a great churchgoer. She was active in St. Patrick's Parish and a committed member of the Catholic Women's League. The CWL had a hospital visiting group and Mother would go at least once or twice a week with her great friend Mrs. Birch to visit the public wards of a large hospital in Montreal. They would bring candies, reading material and food to distribute among the patients.

She helped a great many people in various ways. During the Depression, I can remember Mother often explaining to us why dinner would be a little sparse that evening. It was because she had gladly shared our food with poor people who, earlier in the day, had come to our door hungry. Mother was a kind and generous woman and always set a good example of Christian charity for her children.

Dad was a solid Catholic gentleman. He too was very involved in St. Patrick's Parish and he

Memoirs

devoted much of his time to the St. Vincent de Paul Society. He was also very Irish. In some ways my father was more Irish than the Irishmen in Ireland. He belonged to practically all of the Irish societies including the St. Patrick's Society, and the Unity Club which the men of the parish had founded. In fact, Dad was President of the Unity Club at one time. He was a Hibernian and he also took part in all of the St. Patrick's Day Parades. I do not think he missed a single one until the very end of his life.

In the twenties, during the time of the "troubles" in Ireland, Dad was Vice-President of a local group of the Irish Self-Determination League. When my brother Emmett and I were youngsters, we would be called upon occasionally to perform for them the recitations that we had practiced for our school concerts at Congress Hall or at St. Patrick's. I can remember going to their meetings and singing some Irish song or reciting an Irish poem, much to the delight of the Irishmen present.

During the Depression, my father was an active member of the Trades and Labour Council. He tried to form a union among the employees at the *Montreal Star*. At first the workers seemed very much in favour of the idea, but their enthusiasm soon waned. My dad was fired from the *Star* because of his attempt at "union activity", as they called it. Shocked that Dad's actions had cost him his job, his fellow workers decided to call a protest meeting one afternoon after work. When the time came, however, the only other person at the "meeting" was Arthur Murphy, Dad's great friend and buddy. None of the other workers showed up. Afterwards Dad understood why. The men had been threatened that if they went to the meeting they too would be fired. Obviously, with all the power that Labour now wields, none of this could possibly occur today.

Hearing such stories one can better understand the need for unions. In those days it meant your job to become involved in the labour movement, so my dad was out of work at the height of the Depression, a time when it was virtually impossible to obtain work elsewhere.

That was in the thirties, of course, and Emmett and I were in the Seminary. I had to admire my dad throughout those difficult years. Our family managed to get by until he found a steady job with a private printing firm in Montreal where he worked as a printer until his retirement. Even after retirement Dad would find odd jobs to help support the family, and also, I think, just to keep himself busy for the next several years. Towards the end of his life, he became quite ill. As I look back, I have to say that my appreciation for the character and the constancy and the goodness of that man has grown with time.

My mother and father had eight children, three girls and five boys. Margaret was the oldest in the family, and she, like Mother, lived to a ripe old age. She was eighty-five when she died. Margaret had married in her early thirties. She and her husband, Wilfrid Duggan, had two children, Lenore and Gerald, who were very close to us.

Memoirs

The next child was Irene, who left us at the age of seventeen to enter the Sisters of Providence of St. Vincent de Paul, at their Motherhouse in Kingston, Ontario. Prior to her leaving, there had been some argument at home over whether or not the Sisters would accept her or whether Dad would allow her to go before she was eighteen. After her Profession , Irene would come home occasionally for brief visits, always accompanied by another Sister, as was customary in those days. Those who knew Irene as Sister Mary Lenore are aware that she made quite a reputation for herself as an educator. She was very active in Catholic education groups, and also served as President of the Ontario Teachers' Federation, which was rather exceptional for a Sister at that time.

My brother Cyril was the oldest of the Carter boys. Our parish priest, Father Gerald McShane, who showed a great interest in every student at St. Patrick's, asked Cyril if he ever considered becoming a priest. The following year Father McShane arranged for him to attend Montreal College (Le Collège de Montréal). Before long, however, Cyril decided that the priesthood was not for him. He left the College, found employment and later married. Cyril and his wife Nora had only one child, a son, whom they named Tom.

Then came my brother Tom, my niece Michele's father. He was a great sport and had lots of spirit so he was very popular with the young fellows in the neighbourhood. Wanting to make his own way in life, Tom left home in his teens or early twenties. By strange coincidence, his first job was in Sault Ste. Marie. (I could never have imagined then that I would one day call Sault Ste. Marie Diocese my home. I did not even know where it was.)

The next child was Frankie, who died of pneumonia at just five months of age. Then came Mary. Unlike Irene, Mary decided on her religious vocation later in life. For years she had been associated with the Sisters of the Sacred Heart and had attended their discussion and prayer meetings held each Sunday at the Sacred Heart Convent in Montreal. Mary was twenty-nine when she entered their Community.

I was next in the family, followed three years later by my brother Emmett. We have always been very close, perhaps because we were the youngest of the children. I have admired Emmett's devoted service as priest, educator, Canon, Bishop and Cardinal and I think he has had a profound influence on the Canadian Church.

We had a good family life. There was a pleasant atmosphere in our home, especially in the later years when we were teenagers. Dad and Mother loved music and they were always delighted to have young people in to visit. We would sing and play the piano and enjoy the delicious refreshments that Mother always prepared for us. Those were great times and I have many fond memories.

Memoirs

Our home was always open to guests, especially priests. The Redemptorist Fathers visited often and endeared themselves to our family. We first met the Redemptorists when they were serving as Chaplains at the Christian Brothers' camp which was close to our cottage at Fourteen Island Lake in the Laurentians. They visited with us there during the summer months, and when we were in Montreal they liked to come to our home for a sing-song and a pleasant evening of discussion.

Margaret and Mary and Emmett and myself had a taste for reading. For many years the four of us enjoyed reading good books together and we would take turns at reading aloud. Besides being refreshing, I think this also had a formative influence on us. It is interesting that the books we read were books that had some relation to life and to faith, to our Church and to our society.

As adults, Emmett and I always made time to go home, even though we were leading very busy lives. In the early forties Emmett had the Normal School and the Newman Club and was deeply involved in education around Montreal. My duties at St. Mary's Hospital and the Chancery Office were very demanding; in fact, together they were almost too much for one person. Nonetheless, getting home on Sunday nights was kind of sacred to us. We would be there regularly, unless something absolutely unavoidable prevented it. I think those Sunday evenings we spent together kept us close as a family and were a sign of the love we had for one another. Certainly we had our arguments and sometimes our quarrels - as in most human relationships - but we were always very supportive of one another.

Looking back, I realize that we had an innocent kind of upbringing. Our family life was always very much experienced in relation to the Church. Our Catholic faith was an integral part of our life, not something added, not something we expressed just one day a week. There was definitely an atmosphere of prayer in our home and we would never think of not being at Mass on Sunday. It was understood that Sunday was not only a day of rest, but a day of prayer. Growing up, both Emmett and I were in the Chancel Choir. In fact, as choir boys, we also went to Church every Sunday evening for Benediction, and Mother and Dad would usually accompany us. Then, later on, as students at Montreal College, we went to Mass in the College Chapel on Sundays. So one would have to say that we were raised in a rather old-fashioned Catholic atmosphere, an atmosphere that predominated for the average Irish Catholic family living in Montreal at that time.

During my youth, the city of Montreal was beginning to change dramatically as it grew into a thriving metropolis. The population was growing by leaps and bounds. Vast numbers of French-Canadians were leaving their farms and heading for the city so the society in which we lived quickly became predominantly French-speaking. There was still, however, a sizeable English-speaking population and the French-Canadians had a very simple way of distinguishing us: the English-speaking Catholics were "Les Irlandais", the English-speaking Protestants were "Les Anglais". That was a very neat distinction, though it obviously did not adequately address the reality. Included among Les Irlandais were some good Scots and English, Welshmen and others. These were followed eventually by Italians and other Europeans who had adopted English as their language of business.

The spirit in Montreal, at that time, was very good; at least from our point of view it seemed that way. Because of the existence of some Irish Societies, like the St. Patrick's Society which went back well over a century, English-speaking Catholics, though not terribly strong politically, had at least some influence in the city.

In those days the churches of Montreal were very well attended. Our Catholic people were devout and Sunday Mass was important to them. They also went to Confession regularly - most of them at least once a month, and some of them as often as once a week. The Catholic community of Montreal was, for the most part, a faith-filled and unpretentious population with a deep attachment to their Church.

As I recall those days, I realize that we were living in a very religious society - a very well-organized and tightly controlled society in which the

Church had a great deal of power. Some might say too much power, but this is a matter of debate. I think one could make a case for either side, given the circumstances, the background and the history of that particular time. However, it is not my intention to debate the religious situation in Montreal when I was young, but merely to reflect on my own experience of Church at that time.

My family was very fortunate to have moved into a parish which was probably the best organized and the best managed English-speaking parish in the whole of Montreal and we Carters were very active members. It was there and in the parochial school that most of my Church experience was lived when I was a child.

As parishioners of St. Patrick's we were especially favoured in having a Pastor like Father Gerald McShane. One of the few English-speaking Sulpicians in Montreal, and a tower of strength in the Irish community, he was outstanding for his organizational ability and his intellectual and cosmopolitan understanding of Church. St. Patrick's Church, built in the 1840's for the service of English-speaking Catholics, was the first of the English Churches in Montreal, the Mother-Church really, and Father McShane was appointed Pastor in 1907. This fine priest revolutionized the whole Catholic community and came to be recognized and acknowledged as a true leader by the people he served. He was a man of great ability, and he had a lot of influence, so naturally there were some who

Memoirs

did not like him. There were those who were jealous of him and those who criticized him, but I think that if our family had not been members of St. Patrick's Parish, my life, and perhaps Emmett's as well, would probably have taken a different turn. Father McShane had a profound influence on both of us - an influence which was responsible in some measure for our vocations to the priesthood. I doubt that either of us would have attended Montreal College or pursued our studies for the priesthood if it were not for him. I might add that Father McShane was at St. Patrick's for almost fifty years, so he was our Pastor and advisor from our early days of attending Church until well after our ordination as priests. We were so fortunate to have had the personal help and personal interest of a man of his ability.

I have often reflected on how blessed I was, in those early years, to have had such a close family and to have been part of such a devout parish. Within this setting my formal schooling and the journey which would eventually lead to the Priesthood was begun.

Journey to the Priesthood

My early education was acquired at St. Patrick's School under the direction of the Brothers of the Christian Schools - the De Lasalle Brothers. Many of them were of Irish descent, some having come directly from Ireland. They were renowned as good educators and "no-nonsense" type teachers who instilled in their students a spirit of obedience. You did not argue or answer back. I have to smile when I think of men like Brother Walter, the principal of the school, Brother Raymond and Brother Thomas and so many others who taught us. They were rigid disciplinarians but they were good teachers. Looking back now, despite all the advances in pedagogy, I would have to say that I do not regret having experienced the discipline of the Christian Brothers.

There was sometimes a tendency to be overly strict in those days. That style of discipline would not be accepted today. I can imagine indignant parents and their angry children running to a lawyer to complain of ill treatment. I must say, however, that even if the Brothers were a little too much given to discipline, on the whole, they were reasonable men and fine teachers.

The Brothers were devoted to the individual child and to his education and that devotion was evident not only in the classroom but also in the schoolyard. They joined us for our fifteen-minute periods of recreation and sometimes they played a little soccer with us. The Brothers were also great for handball. We did not have handball courts of the professional type. We played off a single brick wall and we used a tennis ball. Sometimes they would come out after four o'clock to play a game of handball with us for half an hour before we went home. It was during these times that we came to know the Brothers better and grew to appreciate their devotion to us.

I also remember Brother Jerome and his violin classes. I studied violin for a year, but then decided I had no particular talent along that line and gave it up, much to my mother's dismay! Many of the other students, however, began to learn the elements of music and some of them later became accomplished musicians.

I think we have to give full credit to the Christian Brothers. Despite the fact that they did not have the finances or the resources that our schools have today, we received an excellent primary education. I have always kept a very warm and grateful

Memoirs

memory of many of the Brothers who taught me, not only academically, but in other ways as well - particularly by the life that they were leading and the example they were giving us.

The Brothers took their task of teaching Christian doctrine seriously and this certainly had a great influence on us as we were growing up. I remember especially our Catechism classes and our lessons from the old, basic *Butler Catechism*. It is not true to say that we were only drilled in questions and answers, or that religion class was all memory work. We had to prepare our lesson, of course, and Heaven help you if you did not know the answers when the questions were asked - and in the exact words of the Catechism! But, thankfully, the question-and-answer period was over very quickly and for the remainder of the class we had readings from Church history, during which we learned about the Saints of the Church and heard stories of their lives. That part of the class was always fascinating and we became quite engrossed in these stories. Not only did this put a lot of colour into the dry definitions of various parts of the *Butler Catechism*, but I think this also had a great deal to do with my own spiritual orientation later on.

In those days, if young people left school without a religious sense and an understanding of the mystery of our redemption, it certainly was not because of the way we were taught. It was because we ourselves either neglected it or forgot it. When I hear the modern catechists criticizing the old-fashioned and simple way in which religion was taught back then, I always have a little question in my mind. I wonder whether they should be taking as much pride as they seem to do today in the modern methods of teaching religion.

Another element in our education that I recall as being significant was the great respect that the Christian Brothers had for the priests in the parish. We were taught in school to raise our caps whenever we met a priest on the street. (Every young man wore a cap in those days.) This was a regular practice. It was indicative of the respect we had for the priesthood and this attitude of respect probably had some influence on vocations.

I might also add that we were greatly influenced by the fact that, in general, parents were loyal to the school. So, in our family, there was no running home with tales; there was no running home with criticism. If we had any criticism of the Brothers, we kept it to ourselves because we were not encouraged to talk about them in a negative way. The same held true for the clergy. My mother and father certainly had a great respect for the priests in our parish.

***

While the Liturgical ceremonies at St. Patrick's were well celebrated, I do not want to give the impression that I am a "laudator temporis acti" (a praiser of times gone by) concerning the Liturgical observances of the time when I was young. There were certainly abuses that had crept in. For instance, our daily Masses in the parishes were practically always Requiem Masses. One or two cantors who sat near the back of the church (some even reading the newspaper when not singing) would sail through the sung parts of the Mass with great speed and very little interest in a pious or reverential rendering of the lovely words of the Requiem Mass. On the other hand, when things were done well, there is no doubt at all that there were certain attractions about the Latin Liturgy, the pre-Vatican Liturgy, which are not always present in the Liturgy of today.

We must realize, too, that there was no lack of edification at the special paraliturgical celebrations, like the processions on the Feast of Corpus Christi and the Feast of the Sacred Heart. For us, these processions were held at St. Patrick's Congress Grounds. I remember that these services helped us to sense the mystery and the holiness of the Eucharist. The same can be said for some of the "Devotions". Some might criticize the famous Tuesday Devotions to Our Lady of Perpetual Help, but I remember that my sisters attended them regularly and seemed to garner a great deal of value and help from them. I have to say, however, that Sunday Mass was the spiritual highlight of our week.

***

Alex Carter

We were not short of vocations to the priesthood, despite the financial difficulties involved in getting through college in those days. There was no government help. One had to work one's way through college or obtain financial assistance from benefactors. Here again I recall my admiration for our pastor, Father McShane, who supported us in every way. I have often held him up as an example to the priests in our own Diocese of Sault Ste. Marie. I have always maintained that priests are largely responsible for developing an interest in the priesthood, and unless there is a good, solid relationship with a member of the clergy, it is very rare that a young man decides that he wants to be ordained. When I was in the Chancery Office in Montreal, I went through the records one day and learned in detail what I had always known in a general way: Father McShane was responsible for the vocations of about half of the fifty or so English-speaking priests in the Archdiocese of Montreal. That is a tremendous compliment to pay anyone.

Father McShane realized the importance of personal contact in promoting vocations so he regularly visited our school. In the seventh grade he would talk to us about the priesthood. He would announce that he was going over to the Brother Director's office and that he would be there at noon and again at four o'clock. Any boy who felt he had an interest in studying for the priesthood was invited to come and have a talk with him. Well, I succumbed to the invitation. From that moment on, he became extremely interested in my future, with the result that, having completed a two-year Commercial Course, I left St. Patrick's School after eighth grade and went to Montreal College (Le Collège de Montréal) which was maintained and operated by the Sulpician Fathers. Being a Sulpician, Father McShane had a great admiration for French culture. He had done his novitiate in Paris. He spoke beautiful French and had always kept a very close relationship with his Sulpician Community. Besides that, he was convinced that the best form of education for someone preparing for service in the Church was the classical college.

***

Well into the early 1960's in Quebec, the "collège classique" resembled the traditional classical colleges in France. It was definitely an education in the humanities, so it was not particularly suitable for anyone aspiring to be an engineer for example, because the field of mathematics was deemed to be of little importance. The basic courses were French, Greek and Latin authors, History, and the culture of the Church.

I began my studies at the College in 1924. The following year several more English-speaking students enrolled because an English class was opened for the first time. That was when Emmett left St. Patrick's after sixth grade and joined me at the College. We were together throughout our schooling, with Emmett being only one year behind me all the way to Ordination. Our group of friends at that time included Frank Moyle and Johnny Brennan who were neighbourhood chums from St. Patrick's Parish, and Frank McMahon who joined us later from St. Anthony's Parish. We liked to get together often, especially to play sports.

Every day Emmett and I would walk the couple of miles from where we were living to the College and then home again for lunch. In the good weather, we rode our bikes. I do not want to make any invidious comparisons but I cannot help but think that it was probably better for us than being bussed to school both morning and afternoon. It afforded us, first of all, time for companionship and it also gave us some good physical exercise.

While at the College, some of us were junior counsellors at Camp Kinkora, a youth camp which was sponsored by St. Patrick's Parish. I was there for only a year or two. My dad had insisted, much to Father McShane's displeasure, that Emmett and I spend our summer vacations with the family at our summer cottage at Fourteen Island Lake.

The greater number of the students at Collège de Montréal were boarders. As a matter of fact, one of them was Bill Power, who later became Bishop of Antigonish. He was a few years behind us, but we knew him very well and became good friends. Bill's father thought that as a boarder his son would get a better training in French, and he certainly was right. The moment the rest of us left the College grounds we reverted to speaking English.

Memoirs

Those years were fairly exacting. Looking back, however, I have no regrets. We certainly had the advantage of a good French classical education. The College probably provided the best education that was available at that time in Quebec - or perhaps anywhere else for that matter. In fact, many of the leading politicians in Quebec such as Pierre Trudeau, Gérard Pelletier and Jean Marchand were graduates of classical colleges, as were many of the writers, doctors, lawyers and other professional people. You could see it in their logic, in their eloquence and in their ability to communicate.

Of course, one must remember that, in those days, it was very often only one child out of a large family, or at best two or three, that could manage to receive a classical education. The other children were expected to work on the farm or help out at home as soon as they finished elementary school. That is how a professional élite was formed in the province of Quebec. Education was designed, to a large extent, for those who were destined to be lawyers, or doctors or clergy; it was as simple as that. Later, when l'Ecole des Hautes Etudes was founded and the University of Montreal was expanded, economic, financial and social studies gradually became more important.

I have to admit that we English-speaking students were the "spoiled boys" in the College because the Sulpicians had a special regard for us. They let us get away with a lot more than the French-Canadian lads could. No doubt they felt a certain amount of sympathy for these little "Irlandais" who, having barely a working knowledge of the language, were surrounded by French courses, French language and French-Canadian students.

Some elementary French had been taught to us in St. Patrick's, but, in those days, they did not really teach you to speak a language; they primarily taught you the use of verbs, especially the irregular ones. This was not terribly practical since you cannot make a conversation using only verbs, irregular or otherwise! But that was the way things were done when I was a boy and this old-fashioned way of teaching resulted in our having less than a smattering of the French language when we were placed in this French milieu.

It was a struggle in the beginning to get decent marks, but by the time we had reached Belles Lettres and Rhétorique, we were holding our own at the top of the class when it came to examination time. All the Rhétorique students of the Ecclesiastical Province of Montreal who were graduating from the classical colleges competed each year for the Prix Colin. I came in second place. I lost to a student from Collège Sainte Croix in Cartierville.

***

For those studying for the priesthood, it was routine to graduate from Montreal College in

Rhétorique and go on to the Seminary of Philosophy for two years. Once again, we were day scholars and lived at home. Among the Philosophy students were American lads who had been sent to Montreal by their Bishops to study for the priesthood. Some of these Americans brought with them a great spirit of freedom and a certain attitude which was perhaps less disciplined than ours in some ways. They were very endearing, full of fun and good sports. There were several excellent football, baseball and handball players among them. I became very close friends with some of them. One, in particular, Thomas "Tim" Connor became a lifelong friend. Tim was from Wallingford, Vermont. He became ill during his seminary days, and the doctor at the Seminary told him to leave and rest up for a month or two. He had become a good friend of our family and a great favourite of my mother so she was happy to have him come to our home and rest there.

At the mid-term break, Tim and several other American students would come home with us while they were waiting for their evening trains. Mother and Dad would put on a big dinner for them and they would leave, as the time for their trains approached, to go back home, most of them to the New England States. This was the beginning of enduring friendships and I still recall them with great affection.

After Philosophy came the moment of decision. Should I go into le Grand Séminaire ("The Grand" as it was known to the English-speaking students) or should I decide on a different future? Had I been going on for some other profession, I would have had to change direction and go either to McGill or the University of Montreal, or to one of the schools of economics which were in their infancy at that time. However, I had already been fairly well encouraged by the close scrutiny, interest and guardianship of Father McShane. He took it for granted that I would be going into the Seminary of Theology and by that time I had pretty well made up my own mind.

This was the moment of truth, the moment when I decided I would move into the Seminary and take the final steps to the priesthood. I made the decision to apply to the Archdiocese of Montreal, as did my friend Frank Moyle. Since Father McShane was so involved in promoting vocations, he had easy access to the Diocesan Office and the Seminary, so all of the arrangements were made by him. Frank and I were brought down to meet the Archbishop very briefly. He welcomed us, wished us well and then we were directed to report to Father Emile Yelle, the Rector of the Seminary, or the "Superior", as he was called.

It is almost unbelievable to think of it now but there were more than three hundred students of Theology in the Seminary. They came mostly from Montreal and the suffragan dioceses, but also from other dioceses in Canada and the United States. Interestingly enough, we were joined later by several seminarians from the Diocese of Sault Ste. Marie: Henry Murphy, Omer St. Pierre and Regis St. James.

Once again the English-speaking students formed a relatively small group compared to the number of French-speaking students. The twenty or more from the United States, as well as those from Ontario and those from Montreal, gave us ample opportunity for developing friendships. This is not to say that we did not make many friends among the French-speaking seminarians as well. As a matter of fact, one of my closest friends in the Seminary was the future Archbishop of Montreal, Paul Grégoire.

The Rector, Father Yelle, was a very well-known theologian in Quebec and was President at one time of the Thomas Aquinas Association. He was a man of immense qualities. We soon learned that his spiritual lectures were models of discourse based on a deep knowledge of theology and spirituality. He was a great reader and he had a very keen mind. Father Yelle was also quite a disciplinarian. He rarely smiled. Unfortunately he was not with us very long. A year after we went into the Seminary he was chosen to take over the Archdiocese of St. Boniface as Coadjutor Archbishop and Administrator.

In passing I must say that it was a misguided appointment. A man of studies, a man of learning, he was sent to Manitoba into a milieu for which he was unprepared. This man of reflection and study certainly had wisdom, presence and knowledge. However, he did not have the physical stamina necessary for pastoral duties in a Diocese which required so much difficult travel. It was not too long before he became very ill. A few years later, when I met him at the Canadian College in Rome, he told me he was going to resign very shortly and leave St. Boniface. He said, "We are not going to have three sick and retired Archbishops living in St. Boniface." It was most unfortunate. I will always remember him with affection and admiration.

Father Yelle was succeeded as Rector by Father Romeo Lesieur, who was a dear man - a living saint. He followed the law to the letter. He was a disciplined man, a man who I think probably fasted all his life. He certainly gave the impression - in fact, it was obvious - that he was very strict with himself.

I also remember two very old retired French Sulpicians who always walked back and forth together on the grounds of the Seminary. One was a big, tall man, the other very short, and the English-speaking seminarians christened them Dutchie and Sammy. Actually, their names were Duchesne and Gattet, and they had been at the Grand for many years. They did not want to go back to France. They wanted to live out their lives in the Seminary where they had taught for so long. Their very presence was, I think, a kind of blessing to our young spirits because there was almost an other-worldly character about them. They were always smiling and charming when we met them, even though we

Memoirs

knew that they did much penance. Dutchie, for example, would not sit down. He had a high desk and part of his discipline was to stand at the desk and read rather than sit. He would sit down only if someone came to his room to see him. All of these men were fine examples of humility, self-discipline and ascetism.

The Seminary in those days was partly a Novitiate and partly a School of Theology. The Rule that was followed was pretty well the Rule of Jean Jacques Olier, the founder of the Sulpicians. The pertinent parts or the ascetic parts of Olier's Rule were kept in their entirety. They were modified from time to time but no basic change was made in the concept of training, of learning, of ascetic conditions, discipline or prayer life. These were all rolled into one. As a matter of fact, some years before we were there, they had slightly modified the Rule by removing the statement (which always used to be read very seriously) that before entering the chapel the seminarians were to leave their swords at the door. Obviously this had come down through the ages from France and was never changed until it received too many laughs from the seminarians.

Life at the Seminary was undoubtedly an ascetic existence. We followed a strict routine. We were up in the morning at five o'clock for meditation at five-thirty. I will say this for the Sulpician Fathers: they were always present at whatever ceremonies the seminarians were expected to attend.

Alex Carter

Our rooms were small. Our beds were hard. We had running water - we ran and got it! There was a double sink on each floor, and you brought your basin there the night before and filled it up with water. I remember that sometimes when there was an east wind blowing and the temperature was below zero, I would have to crack a little glaze of ice from the basin before shaving. As I say, it was certainly an ascetic existence.

Because of the number of students it was difficult for the Seminary to serve meals that satisfied everyone, especially since we came from such diverse backgrounds. There were some health problems for a few years because we were all very fatigued and several of the students actually became ill. As a result, some of the Bishops from the United States became concerned and one or two in particular stopped sending their students to Montreal.

As seminarians, we were not allowed to go into the city at all unless it was to see our own doctor or dentist. (A doctor did come to the Seminary once a week.) Our only outings were walks, which were just as much a sacrifice as staying in, because we had to go out in large groups. Twenty or thirty young men walking in cassocks naturally attracted a lot of attention on the streets of Montreal, not always pleasant or flattering at that. Whenever I was in charge of a walk, I would head for the mountain. I lead my group off the streets of Montreal as fast as I could and climbed up the mountainside. Mind you, when I reported to Father Lesieur after our walk, he would always give me a little half-smile and tell me he certainly hoped that none of us had been smoking!

Theology was, of course, the theology of St. Thomas Aquinas. There was no question about the fact that Thomism was the basis of all the theology taught in the Grand Seminary at that time. We had some teachers who were excellent theologians. They had drawn up courses from their own doctoral studies and they gave us a teaching that was culled from the best of theological sources. We had received an excellent course on Grace. Obviously we had studied the renowned quarrels of the Dominicans and the Jesuits on that subject. We also had good lecturers brought in for talks at the Seminary and some of them were excellent, even exciting! In particular, I remember when the great Dominican theologian, Father Marie-Dominique Chenu came. He was then, even in November 1932, becoming a bone of contention because of what some were calling "Modernism" in his theological teachings. He gave us an outstanding talk in which he criticized the simplistic way we had of rejecting other theological opinions by giving a very poor summary and then refuting it. He suggested that very often we built up a straw man, destroyed it, and then went on to present our own thesis as being the proper one and the only one. That was, I think, when I began to realize the complexity of Theology and to realize that there were many schools of thought. Given the times in which we lived, I would have to say our courses in Theology were adequate.

Some of our courses could have been better, however. For example, I do not think the liturgical studies were up to par. Liturgy was mostly ritual and there seemed to be too much stress on the ceremonies rather than the meaning and the beauty of the Liturgy. Scripture was taught in an extremely conservative way, as was Church History. In fairness though, I must say that the great advances of knowledge and research in these fields were in their infancy at that time. We are going back, remember, to the thirties.

There was certainly no great effort to give us any practical experience for our future priestly ministry. The contention was, as I heard it expressed by the Sulpicians now and then, that the students had to receive their spiritual formation first, and the only time that could be done was during the years in the Seminary. They maintained that if you were well based in theology and well disciplined and trained in what the priesthood is and what it represents, then your pastoral experience would be acquired easily. It would develop as you practised priestly ministry, under the guidance of your pastor, or through whatever assignment or charge you might be given by your Bishop. Now this may sound like a simplistic approach to us today, and we could debate this question forever, but I think that somewhere along the line there is a happy medium. I am not sure that we have reached it even today.

Memoirs

All in all, I have no basic complaint with my seminary days. Naturally we beefed and complained every now and then. We did not accept everything "bouche béante" (with our mouths open). We had our moments of annoyance when we felt some things were petty. We felt that it was not necessary to rise at five in the morning and retire at nine o'clock at night all year long. Our only break was after the semester at the end of January, which was about a ten-day or two-week holiday, and then we were back in classes again until the end of June. We certainly did not have much contact with the outside world during that time. As I said before, it was almost unheard of to get permission to leave the Seminary for a rest unless one was too sick to be looked after or had a breakdown or something of that nature.

Somewhere around the third year I went through a period of fatigue. I suppose today they would call it "burn-out". The doctor advised me to try to take things easy for the next few months. He suggested I try to get out on the grounds rather than stay in my room and also to take a little extra nourishment. To do that, of course, I had to have the permission of the Superior because as part of our ascetic training we were not allowed to have food in our rooms. So I went to see Father Lesieur, who was very kind and very generous. He gave me permission to have some fruit in my room to help me regain my strength. The weariness eventually passed and there were no ill effects from it.

Alex Carter

The years in the Seminary passed very quickly. I had received all of my calls to Orders. In student language that meant I was never "clipped", or denied a call, which was a warning that your conduct was not "right up to scratch" or that your examination results were below standard. (They would tell you the reason why you were clipped.) Everyone on the Faculty voted upon each call to Orders, except, of course, one's spiritual director who had to remain silent during the debate.

Each year, six deacons - so-called "Deacons of Honour" - were ordained six months earlier than their classmates. I was chosen to be one of them. We were to serve as deacons at the Solemn High Mass at the Seminary, the House of Philosophy, Montreal College, the Cathedral or the two Sulpician Churches of Notre Dame and St. Jacques le Majeur. I was assigned to Notre Dame. I enjoyed very much the beauty of that church and the magnificent music of the Liturgies there.

***

I was ordained to the priesthood on June 6th, 1936 at St. James Cathedral in Montreal by Auxiliary Bishop Alphonse-Emmanuel Deschamps, along with some one hundred classmates. I celebrated my first Mass the following day in St. Patrick's Church, assisted by my pastor, Father Gerald McShane, who very proudly stood next to me at the eleven o'clock Mass. I had been choir boy, altar server and usher at St. Patrick's during my

Memoirs

school and college days, all of which made the moment more meaningful. It was in every sense a true celebration. An ordination, even in this modern day with its critical approach to everything, is still a moving experience that our people seem to understand in a profound way and which brings joy to the community.

It is one of the good signs of our Church today that our people are still so proud and so happy to greet a newly ordained priest. I think this is a sign of hope. Without gainsaying any of the very real and important steps that we took in Vatican Council II for the priesthood of the laity, there is no question at all that the sacramental reality of the ministerial priesthood is extremely important to the life of the Church.

After my ordination I was sent by Archbishop Georges Gauthier to replace the Chaplain of St. Patrick's Orphanage for the summer months. I spent a very pleasant summer there with the youngsters, playing ball with them and taking them around town whenever possible. I was then appointed an assistant at St. Anthony's Parish in Montreal - a parish which included the very well-to-do business people who lived on the hill near Lord Shaugnessy's home, and the relatively poor working people who lived below the hill.

Shortly after my arrival at St. Anthony's, I was told that Archbishop Gauthier also wanted me to serve as a Notary on the Marriage Tribunal. I was to

Alex Carter

go to the Chancery Office two or three times a week to help out with marriage cases. My ministry at St. Anthony's and the Tribunal, however, turned out to be short-lived. It was just a year later that I was called in by the Archbishop and informed that he wanted me to go to Rome to study. This came as a bit of a shock because I do not think there had been an English-speaking priest sent to Rome from Montreal for something like twelve years. As an example of how things were done in those days, I would like to recount my audience with the Archbishop. It is too good to be ignored!

Archbishop Gauthier said to me, "My son, I want you to go to Rome for two years to take post-graduate courses. What would you like to study?"

When I told him that I would really like to study philosophy, the Archbishop shook his head and said, "No! I do not intend to appoint you to a University or College. I do not think that would best serve the interests of the Diocese."

"Well, what about theology?" I asked. "I like theology very much. In fact, I would not mind teaching."

"No," said the Archbishop, "I do not think that you should be going into a Seminary to teach. You know, I really need someone to help with the Marriage Tribunal. We have quite a backlog of marriage cases. They are coming in rapidly and I think the situation is going to get even worse. What we really need is a canon lawyer. So I think you should study Canon Law."

Thus having been given my choice, I ended up receiving a mandate to study Canon Law because, obviously, that was the Archbishop's intention from the very beginning. He was trying to be very considerate and very gentle by asking me for my preference, but in the final analysis what he was actually doing was telling me: "You are going to Rome to study Canon Law."

New Horizons

I had some compunction about leaving for Rome in 1937 because Canada was in the throes of the Depression and my family had been affected by it. This was my only concern and I explained to the Archbishop that I wanted to be of some help to my parents. The Archbishop assured me that he had other plans which would relieve me of this worry. I presume he was thinking that Emmett would be ordained soon and he would be able to help if the family were in great need.

In those days, you were given a mandate to go and study, but you were not given any salary during your absence from the Diocese or any travelling expenses. The Archbishop had told me that there were bursaries available at the Canadian College - the residential college which the Sulpicians had established for Canadian student priests in Rome - and he would ask that one of them be allotted to me. He also suggested that I speak to Father McShane. Father McShane, who had heard from the

Archbishop about his plans for me, said that he would gladly supply me with my steamship fare from his own fund. Moreover, Monseigneur Albert Valois, a good friend who was Chancellor of the Archdiocese of Montreal, assured me that he would see to it that I received a number of Mass Stipends regularly. Each Mass Stipend was fifty cents, but in those days even fifty cents was a big help.

What really overwhelmed me, however, was the generosity of the people of St. Anthony's Parish. I was particularly fortunate in having met people of such profound faith. Parish visitation, which was a common practice in those days, had been a delight for me. Everywhere I went I received a heartfelt welcome and their love for the priest was so manifest. There are many difficult things about the service of the priesthood, but I do not think very many people receive the real, objective love that a young priest receives in his first parish, if he is dedicated to the service of the parishioners. By the time the parishioners, particularly those from below the hill, came to my assistance, I had enough money to set out for further studies with no hesitation. I have rarely seen a greater expression of gratitude and generosity anywhere. After all, they had known me less than a year. It was a very touching experience, and I have never forgotten it.

For one brought up in the Sulpician tradition and in the ultramontane Church that existed at that time, it was rather exciting to be sent to Rome to study. When I say ultramontane I am not necessarily qualifying all of the Montreal or Quebec traditions in the late thirties as being ultra-conservative and right-wing. There is no doubt at all, however, that we had a very simplistic training on the role of the Church, the role of the bishop, the role of religious, and the role of the people in the Church. Church authority was very highly respected and we were expected to obey without any question. It was with a very strong devotion to the Holy See that young priests in those days approached the prospect of going to the Holy City to delve into the history and the life of the Church from a closer perspective.

In those days there were no airplanes jetting thousands of people across the ocean every day. It took a week to go by boat and the number of tourists was very small. How different today with world travel now taken for granted by millions of people! Since my previous out-of-country travel had been limited to short trips to the United States, the voyage was an exciting and charming experience for me. After a delightful cruise on an Italian ship out of New York, with several stops along the way, including the Azores, I landed in Naples. There I remained for a few days to get my bearings before going on to Rome.

***

Arriving at the Canadian College on the via delle Quattro Fontani I was warmly welcomed by the Rector, Monseigneur Léonidas Perrin, a friendly and quiet Sulpician Father who had been in Rome for a long time and was highly respected at the Vatican. Soon I was reunited with two of my old friends from the Seminary, Laurent Morin and Armand Racicot, who were already studying in Rome. Laurent later became Auxiliary Bishop of Montreal and then in 1959 he was appointed Bishop of Prince Albert, Saskatchewan. Armand became a Canon in the Diocese of St. Jean (now St. Jean - Longeuil) and his untimely death after the war would deprive the Church of a very fine and very talented priest. Racicot had always been one of the great entertainers at the Seminary. He had a magnificent voice. He knew many of the old familiar French-Canadian songs and very often led in the celebrations held at different times by the seminarians.

It was good to meet other young priests from different parts of Canada. The experience was almost a return to the days of the Seminary, except that the setting was completely different and we were now doing post-graduate studies. There were also many more distractions because the grandeur, the beauty and the complexity of Rome were there waiting to be discovered, examined, scrutinized and enjoyed.

Just a few days after my arrival, I had my first glimpse of Pope Pius XI. Our Retreat was finished and this was the day we were to report for the opening of classes at the Institute of Canon Law. Originally, the Appolinaris College, near the Piazza Navona, had housed the Institute, but that day the

Holy Father was arriving to bless the new building which had been erected for it near St. John Lateran. The students were naturally called upon to attend the opening. The presence of Pius XI made the occasion all the more memorable for us! I think, for any Catholic, seeing the Pope in person for the first time is always a powerful experience, since the Holy Father is, for us, the centre of unity in the Church.

This was also my first introduction to the free and easy discipline of Roman groups. We had been standing around very peacefully outside the entrance when the limousine appeared. As the Pope and his attendants descended from the vehicle and went into the new building, there was instant pandemonium and a few hundred young men tried to get through the door at the same time! I remember Morin, Racicot and myself having to lock arms so that we would not be pulled apart as we forced our way into the building. We found a seat in the big hall and listened as the Pope gave his address and ended by blessing us and the new building.

Not being attracted to a study limited solely to the legislation of the Church, I was very happy to discover, as I began my classes in Canon Law, that there was a much broader field of erudition and knowledge encompassed in the course. I enjoyed the History of Law and the Philosophy of Law. Most of all, I enjoyed the study of Roman Law. It was more fascinating in its depth than English or Germanic Law and one could not help but realize the extent to which Roman law has influenced legislation over the centuries. There is an old saying that "The Romans are born jurists." They probably needed to be since, at the time of the Roman Empire, they controlled so much of the world.

We had some very practical teachers. Several had experience in the legislation of the Church through their work in the Vatican Offices and Congregations. I remember specifically and with great gratitude, the classes of Francesco Roberti in "De Processibus", the legal trials conducted by the tribunals of justice in the Church. He was a magnificent professor but one had to pay absolute attention because he spoke Latin very, very quickly. In fact he did everything quickly! His lectures were always beautifully prepared. He did not use notes. Speaking a mile a minute he went through the forty-five minutes of his lecture, then took off, leaving us with a host of quickly jotted-down notes dealing with canonical procedures that had been set in place by the Church over many years. Roberti later became a Cardinal and at the Council was chosen by Pope Paul VI to be head of the Commission for the Reform of the Roman Curia. From a pedagogical point of view, I would not say that he was a good teacher but he was a very learned man.

Pedagogically, the best teacher we had was the well-known Belgian Capucin, Father Gommarius Michiels, who was rated at that time as one of the great canonists. If our *Code of Canon Law* had not been revised, I would think that his book *De Personis* would remain perhaps the finest work of its kind. He was much more personal than most of the professors. Father Michiels made it a point to know us individually. He took an interest in each of us, despite the fact that he had a large assembly to address each morning, and he and I became quite friendly.

Some years later Father Michiels was invited by Cardinal Rodrigue Villeneuve, Archbishop of Quebec to teach a summer course in Canon Law at Laval University. While Michiels was in Quebec City, he got in touch with me and came to Montreal where he was my guest for a few days. During our visit, Father Michiels and I discussed the complexities of legislation on sterilization and various other problems of medical ethics that were then just beginning to receive public attention. As I recall, we agreed at that time that simplistic answers were sometimes given in cases where complex situations required consideration of other values. It is interesting to note that many of the questions we were discussing then are still with us today and that we have not solved all of the challenges that their complexity offers. Later on, during our debates in the Canadian Catholic Conference (CCC), now renamed the Canadian Conference of Catholic Bishops (CCCB), I often thought of those days when I had sat and listened to Michiels. Even though he was fairly strict in his interpretation of the teaching of the Church, he showed profound awareness of the complexity of human situations. He realized it is not always possible to solve life's problems with a simple yes or no answer.

Alex Carter

Among our professors were some excellent laymen who brought with them a wealth of knowledge and experience. They were legal specialists. Some were doctors "utriusque juris", that is, with degrees in both Civil and Canon Law. They were highly qualifed lawyers who pleaded cases in the civil courts as well as in the Sacred Roman Rota. Just a few years before, discussions had gone on between the Holy See and the government of Mussolini. These had led to a settlement of the "Roman Question". Some of the properties taken over by the government of Italy were restored to the Holy See and sums of money were paid to reimburse the Church for the many properties which the government had appropriated. These lawyers had played a very important role in this process.

***

We had a fine group of students at the Canadian College. They were friendly and the spirit was excellent. We had many pleasant and entertaining gatherings during our evenings together, some of them up on the roof in the good weather. I must say that I was fascinated with Rome. We visited many of the different historical sites, churches and shrines both in the city and in the surrounding areas. One of my classmates, Frank Scott from Chatham, New Brunswick, had a keen interest in history. He became familiar with the legends, stories and facts about different Roman buildings as well as the habits and customs of the Romans. So, he became our guide. Almost every day - certainly four or five days a week at least - we would decide which particular shrine or historical site we wanted to visit. Scotty proved to be a veritable gem as he familiarized us with those ancient places of interest and made each Roman outing a worthwhile endeavour. I doubt that I would have acquired one-third of my knowledge of Rome had Scotty not been with us.

One of my most compelling memories of Rome was the visit of Hitler. It was early in May 1938, at the time of the famous pact between Mussolini and himself. Prior to this visit, Pope Pius XI had opposed Hitler vocally many times. On one occasion, the Holy Father had given a speech on the radio, telling the people not to listen to Hitler. The Fascist authorities had cut him off in the middle of his speech and the radio went completely dead. Now, in protest of Hitler's visit, and furious at the very thought of him coming to Rome, the Pope ordered the closing of all the Ecclesiastical Colleges and he retired to his country retreat, Castel Gondolfo.

When Hitler did arrive, we went to have a look, just out of curiosity. It was evident that the big celebrations were not successful at all. As Hitler made his way to the Piazza Venezia, the streets were lined with Fascist troops and only a scattering of people. Most Roman citizens stayed at home, thus voting with their feet. Listening to the Holy Father, they did not give Hitler a warm or enthusiastic reception.

Again, one evening, I watched from a distance as Hitler addressed the Facist troops and a few ordinary citizens at the Quirinale, the former palace of the Pope, which had been turned into a military centre. On one side of him was a life-sized statue of St. Peter and on the other side was a life-sized statue of St. Paul. This was certainly an ironical setting for the kind of ranting and hatred that was being spewed forth from the lips of that man.

After Pius XII became Pope in March 1939, there were also disagreements between him and Mussolini. One of these was on the occasion when Mussolini ordered the storekeepers along the main streets downtown to put up signs which read "No Jews Allowed". As we walked through the streets, we saw many signs placed in the doorways of the small stores that catered to tourists. That same day, the Pope made an appeal to the Roman people asking them not to put up those signs, or if they had already done so, to take them down. We returned the following day and practically all of the signs, certainly seventy-five percent of them, had disappeared. So when you hear so much talk about the Pope not doing anything during the war, you realize that this was mostly propaganda. We might question whether he could have spoken out more directly during that time, but we must take into consideration the calculated risk that any such action would have had. As for the action or non-action of Pius XII, it is something that one would like to reflect more about and probably study further. However, I do think that, at last, we are coming to the point where his role is better understood and more honestly described than it was in some of the literature written a few years ago about his Pontificate. Recent research has shown that the Pope secretly and quietly encouraged the hiding of thousands of Jewish people during the occupation of Rome. One of the men responsible for this clandestine activity was Monsignor Hugh O'Flaherty, who returned to Rome in January 1938 and worked as a secretary in the Holy Office, a few feet from St. Peter's Basilica. I knew him well and we often had tea and strawberry shortcake together at the nearby Pensione Suisse.

Later, during the war, O'Flaherty had a "secret railroad" going practically into the Vatican. There was nothing that the Nazis were able to do about it. (The story of that "railroad" has been made into a television film, *The Scarlet and the Black,* though it is not necessarily exact.) O'Flaherty would dress victims of the Nazi terror in cassocks and in his own second-hand soutane to bring them into Vatican City, where he hid them until it was safe to get them out. He is credited with saving a great number of people.

Those were days when you saw much heroism by people who took great chances. There were some among our close friends in Rome who would put their heads on the block in order to help many of these desperate people who were being searched out and persecuted.

While I was in Rome the dictatorship of Mussolini was beginning to create difficulties. This was the time of the Ethiopian conquest by Italy and of Mussolini's other claims to the whole of the Mediterranean, which he called Mare Nostrum. They were, from that point of view, exciting days but they were also very worrisome days. As students, we went many times out of curiosity to listen to Il Duce in the Piazza Venezia. It was really frightening to see the depth of the acclaim and the hypnotic control that he could have over the crowds. Even the wildest of statements brought cheers and caused great excitement amidst that mass of thousands and thousands of people gathered to hear him. Many of them were Fascists who obviously had been mobilized. They were told to be there and they had no choice. They would have been in trouble had they not shown up. Regardless of how artificial all of this may have seemed to us, one could not help but sense the depth of feeling that can be aroused in a crowd. I have never forgotten that.

I was not an Italian, so I could be much more detached about Mussolini's speeches. I must say though, that one did experience, at times, a sense of excitement. When the crowd was becoming hysterical, with everyone shouting "Viva Il Duce!", something like an electric energy went through your system. You almost wanted to be one of the crowd. You felt as though you would like to belong. And you had to exercise an act of the will not to allow yourself to be caught up in, or to show approval for, something which you could not accept morally. It

Memoirs

was rather a humbling experience and it shows that we are subject to many influences which are not always clearly discernable.

A German priest told me about a similar experience he had had with Hitler in Germany. He was a loyal German, but he said that he was frightened by the hypnosis that seemed to penetrate the crowds gathered to see and hear that madman. He told me that when Hitler spoke, everything Hitler was saying was alien and offensive to him. Yet when that almost electric impulse of emotion went through the crowd, he would be physically inclined to raise his arm and cry out, "Heil Hitler!" and applaud, putting aside his rational opposition to the words that he was hearing. That experience was extremely frightening for him as well.

***

Of all the notable leaders of Church and State in whose presence I found myself during my years as a student in Rome, Pope Pius XI holds a special place in my memory. My first personal contact with him was on February 2, 1938. Those priests who have studied in Rome will remember that it was the custom of the national Colleges to send two students to present the candle that had been blessed on Candlemas Day to the Holy Father. Racicot and myself were designated to present the candle on behalf of the Canadian College. Naturally, the Holy Father was very kind and said a few words to each one of us on that occasion.

However, our most striking meeting with him took place the following year at a special audience held during the 50th anniversary celebrations of the Canadian College. It is one that I still remember vividly. The Pope was eighty-one and had been very ill, so we were not sure that the audience would be possible. It was cleared at the last moment, however, and all of the priests of the Canadian College, led by Monseigneur Perrin, went to see Pius XI. He was visibly weakened. Every now and then, the eyes would flash and a little of his old vigour would come back, but this strong man, who had been an Alpine climber and who usually looked so powerful, was obviously in physical pain. He would slump a little in the chair and then pull himself up again as he gave us a most striking talk. It was not very long, but it was very prophetic. He said something like this:

"You are the young priests who have come to Rome. You are going back to Canada and will continue to build the Church there. I do not place any limits on the providence of God, but I am sure that my life expectancy is very short. I want you to take this message away with you. The Church, the mystical Body of Christ, has become a monstrosity. The head is very large, but the body is shrunken. You, the priests, must rebuild that body of the Church and the only way that you can rebuild it is to mobilize the lay people. You must call upon the lay people to become, along with you, the witnesses of Christ. You must call them especially to bring Christ back to the workplace, to the marketplace."

Memoirs

This powerful message was like a Last Will and Testament of the Pope. As a matter of fact that was his last public audience. All audiences were cancelled the following day and he died not long afterwards. From the beginning of his Pontificate, Pius XI was the Pope of Catholic Action. He was the one who had often written to the Bishops of the world, calling for the participation of lay people in the work of evangelization. Thus it was in keeping with his own teaching that he gave us his last message - a message from the grave, you could almost say. The memory of the moment remains with me. I can visualize it, even now, in my old age. I have never forgotten that audience and as a matter of fact, I believe that it has shaped, in part, my own life and my approach to my role as Pastor, Chaplain and Bishop.

***

Pius XI died in early February 1939, and the sad news spread quickly through Rome. On that occasion I was reminded that the Italians have a special brand of wit that endures even in the most serious and grave circumstances. Pius XI, being from Northern Italy, had brought quite a few Milanese to Rome to staff some of the Offices of the Vatican where he wanted a little more energetic performance. The news of his death had just been announced when an Italian Monsignor visiting at the Canadian College said to the three or four of us standing there, "Well, Pius XI has died so there is going to be a new street in Rome. It is going to be called 'Via Milanesi' ('Out, all the Milanese!')."

Naturally, on hearing of the death of the Holy Father, we headed for the Vatican. I was in St. Peter's Square where many people had gathered and I met Archbishop Joseph Guillaume Forbes of Ottawa, who was visiting at the Canadian College. I said, "Have you gone in to pay your last respects to the Holy Father?"

"Oh, no, we cannot do that now," he said. "The body has not been brought down for the wake yet."

I said, "You are the Archbishop of Ottawa. You could get in, I am sure, if you wanted to."

"I would not know where to go."

"Well, do you want me to go with you?" I offered.

The dear old man said, "Yes, I would love that, if you think there is any possibility."

"Sure there is!" I assured him. "You will be saluted by the guards as you go along. Just acknowledge their salute and we will go upstairs. Then we'll see what happens."

We had just reached the Pope's apartment when we were stopped by some guards who were standing by the door. I said, "This is the Archbishop of Ottawa and he would like to come in for a moment to pay his last respects and say a prayer." They said "Bene" and we walked in - right into the

Pope's bedroom! His body was still on the bed. The Archbishop of Ottawa had just finished praying when we heard a great commotion in the corridor outside the bedroom so we decided to leave. The Camerlingo, Cardinal Eugenio Pacelli, was arriving with all his attendants and companions to make the final statement that the Pope was dead and that his body could now be released. There were a few curious looks in our direction from those who were with the Cardinal as they marched past us into the Pope's room. We walked on quietly, down the stairs and out onto St. Peter's Square. It was obvious that Archbishop Forbes was thrilled to have actually been at the Pope's bedside.

Later that evening, the various Colleges housing priests and seminarians from the different nations of the world took turns at spending an hour's vigil in the chapel where Pope Pius XI was being waked. I think the time of our vigil was one o'clock in the morning. It was very late anyway. The next day we assisted at the funeral. Those were sad days in a way, and yet there was so much beautiful ceremony surrounding the Pope's death. Our presence and participation in this memorable event had been an unexpected and touching experience.

In the interval between the death of Pius XI and the election of Pius XII, there was a distinct effort made to stop the election, or the possible election, of Cardinal Pacelli. The power play reminded me of the way Popes were elected in the old days. The great Roman families used to war with one another, trying to stack the votes in favour of one old family over another. At that time, countries used to send their delegates and ambassadors to try to influence the choice of the new Pontiff. The same kind of effort actually happened between the time of the death of Pope Pius XI and the coming of the Cardinals. In fact, it was started by Mussolini and Hitler. The Fascist and Nazi parties, using their newspapers in Italy and Germany, started a campaign to convince people that Pacelli would not be acceptable as Pope. I saw some of these articles myself. The effort was to no avail, of course.

It was after the third ballot in the afternoon that we saw the white smoke, signalling that a new Pope had been elected. Suddenly the people started cheering. It was an electrifying moment, especially when Cardinal Ottaviani appeared on the balcony and announced "Habemus Papam" ("We have a Pope"). I remember the lady standing next to me being so happy when Ottaviani uttered the word "Eugenio", that she and a few other Italians around us started to scream, "He is a Roman! He is a Roman!" They did not even wait to hear "Pacelli", despite the fact that Cardinal Tisserant's name was also Eugene. They were delighted to have one of their own. Then the new Pope came out and gave his blessing - "Urbi et Orbi" ("To the City and to the World"). It was a moment of triumph, I think, because of the opposition that had come from the dictators. It was a reassertion of the independence of the Church whose members did not have to bow to and accept the power of those who seemed to be able to bully even the strongest of countries. We witnessed here the freedom of the Christian and Catholic people. It was an act of courage on the part of the Cardinals at that time to refuse to be influenced unduly by these powerful dictators.

At the Coronation ceremony I was fortunate to have a good place, as I acted as secretary to Bishop Martin Johnson, who had come over from Nelson, B.C. for his *ad limina* visit. I had been writing a series of articles for his diocesan paper, *The Prospector*, at the request of Father Radey McKenna, whose task this had been until he completed his studies and left Rome. The Bishop had also sent me his quinquennial report, asking me to translate it into Latin. He picked up this report when he arrived in Rome and asked if I would act as his secretary at the Coronation of Pius XII. I was happy, of course, to do so.

It was, as usual, a typical Roman celebration, with much pomp and ceremony. All of the students at the Canadian College were happy about the choice of Pope because Pacelli had attended the 50th anniversary dinner at the Canadian College and he had talked to each one of us. As a result, we felt that we knew him personally so it was rather special for us to see this new Pope coming into office.

As I write this, I recall what a poor press Pius XII had after his death and how unfairly he has been treated. In many ways he was not recognized for the contribution he had made during his

Pontificate. He had helped to set the stage for Vatican II by making changes that prepared the way for the Council. He started changing age-old customs when they were no longer practical or applicable. An example of this was the Eucharistic fast. At that time, not even a drop of water was to be taken after midnight in preparation for the reception of Holy Communion the following morning. That rule was becoming almost impossible for some people to follow. I know I suffered from it myself, especially later on when I returned to Montreal and was Chaplain of St. Mary's Hospital. Sometimes I would receive a sick call at two o'clock in the morning. My throat would be as dry as a chip, and I could not even take a sip of water. Occasionally I might be called again a few hours later. It was a regulation which was not based on reality. Although there were indults given to certain groups and individuals, the old law stood as it was and you were expected to keep it to the letter. Pius XII was the one who changed some of these formerly "unchangeable" rules and regulations.

The encyclical, *Divino Afflante Spiritu*, which impressed me very much when I read it shortly after it came out in 1943, has to be the highlight of what Pius XII contributed. It opened up research in Scripture to Catholic scholars who at that time were running into difficulties with the insistence of the Holy Office upon a kind of automatic fundamentalism. Vatican II would have been impossible if that situation had continued to exist in the Church.

***

Memoirs

The two years I spent in Europe passed very quickly. In the thirties, students usually took advantage of the Easter holidays and the long period between classes from June to mid-October, to see some of Europe. It certainly was a great opportunity to travel, even if we had to do so on very little money.

Like most Roman students I took a trip to the Holy Land during the Easter holiday. I went with Father Laurent Morin, and we had a delightful time. Even in those days this trip made one aware of the long-term misunderstanding and enmity between the Jewish and Arab peoples. When we landed at Haifa, we were told by British soldiers that the road we planned to take was closed due to fighting between the Jews and the Arabs, so we had to take another route. Later, on Good Friday, we had gone down to mid-town Jerusalem, walking through the gate and around the Way of the Cross. As we were heading back, once again some British soldiers stopped us and told us we could not possibly return by that road. They said there was very serious fighting and some shooting and they were surprised that we had been able to get as far as we did. We had to leave Jerusalem through a different gate and go around the city to get back to the Franciscan monastery where we were staying. Obviously the troubles that are prevalent there today have a long, long history and it will take a great deal of help from many quarters before some kind of enduring peace and understanding are reached.

Later on in that year of 1938, I made a trip to Budapest for the World Eucharistic Congress. Three other priests from the Canadian College and I joined an Italian pilgrimmage and went by train. It took forty-eight hours each way with eight of us packed into a small compartment. Even though it was physically exhausting, it was a wonderful experience to visit this magnificent city and attend the Congress itself. What struck me most about the Congress was the deep, sincere, almost passionate devotion of the Hungarian people to the Blessed Sacrament.

I still think that the best trip of my life was through Europe with my fellow students Father Frank Scott and Father George Childs at the end of the first year of our studies in Rome. Most of us at the Canadian College did not have enough money to travel for three or four months so we had to find ways of earning the necessary funds. Scotty and George offered their services to a Scottish diocese. That was the way most of the English-speaking students did it. The Scots were always looking for help from the Canadian College. As for me personally, I had followed Radey McKenna, once again at his recommendation, to become the Chaplain to the Duke and Duchess of Caffarelli and their family, at their summer home in Borselli.

The stay at the Caffarelli home was an education in itself. Their daughter-in-law, Donna Maria and her four children were living with their grandparents, the Duke and Duchess, during the sum-

Memoirs

mertime. I was very much impressed by the knowledge these youngsters had of languages. Their native Italian, naturally, they spoke perfectly. Their mother spoke elegant French, German and English. The secret to the success of the children's education, I discovered, was that they would have a German governess for two or three years, then an English governess for the same period of time. French was spoken quite often in the home by their mother, so they learned French as well.

When I was there, the governess was an English lady. There were certain days when I was instructed by the Duchess that because this was their English day, the children must speak English at all times. At table you had to give them a cold look if they happened to ask for something in Italian. The amazing thing was that those youngsters, aged fourteen, twelve, eight and six, all spoke very good English.

The surroundings were fantastic. Borselli was a lovely little town about forty miles or so from Florence and about ten miles from Valombrosa, which revives memories of Dante and of his *Divine Comedy*, which he actually composed there. It was also somewhat of a throw-back to the Middle Ages. The Duke and Duchess owned the land that was parcelled out to farmers to be cultivated.

In my spare time, I would go for walks, or take my bike and ride to Valombrosa, or take the bus into Florence every now and then. Sometimes I liked to visit the local farmers and chat with them. By this time I knew enough Italian to be able to express myself and to understand most of what was being said. During my conversations with these people, I did not get the impression of any resentment on their part. They worked the land and accepted the Duke and Duchess as the Lord and Lady of the Manor. If there was any resentment, or sense of being victimized, it certainly did not show. I am not saying that this was necessarily a common thing all over Italy at the time, but certainly around Borselli that was the case. Towards the end of August, when the Caffarelli family left for the Adriatic where they had another summer home, I went to Scotland to join my two friends, Scotty and George, and we embarked upon our tour of Ireland and Europe.

We used a list of *pensiones* that had been prepared by former students - also impoverished - who had gone to the Canadian College before us. It was marvelous to be able to find these well-recommended and fine people with small *pensiones* in Italy and France and Belgium or wherever else we went, including Ireland. It was a way of travelling which brought us into much closer contact with the people. Today you can travel through Europe and feel that you have not left your own country - just going from hotel to hotel. In those days we enjoyed outdoor operas in the cheap seats, outdoor symphony performances, and the galleries and museums of the big cities of Europe. It was the best way to learn firsthand about a country.

Memoirs

Our trip to Ireland in 1938 was my first journey to the home of my ancestors. We visited the various places in Ireland that were of interest to us. One *pensione* we stayed in had housed the Irish rebels during the time of the Black and Tans. We were shown the secret steps and basement by which the rebels would escape when the Black and Tans would drive up to the door and raid the house, suspecting that the leading Irishmen might be meeting there. Michael Collins, who was the most popular of the great Irish patriots, used that spot as one of his hiding places when he was being hunted by the Black and Tans. It was during that horrible time when the British government opened prisons and sent cut-throats to fight against the Irish who were struggling for the Irish Republic. Anyhow, we were housed with a very patriotic Irish rebel family. I was impressed by the stories of their adventures and the stories of the troubled times.

Another interesting experience was the Gaelic football final between Galway and Kerry. I had never seen an Irish football game. We think our football is rough in the American or the Canadian Football Leagues. Believe me, it is nothing compared to Gaelic football! They do not wear any pads and yet it is a murderous attack. If you are hurt and carried off the field, you cannot be replaced. It was quite a game! There were about forty thousand people in Dublin for this event, which was the final for all of Ireland. Before the game we all rose to our feet and sang "Faith of Our Fathers", followed by the Irish national anthem, "Soldiers Are We". Then

Bishop Brown of Galway came out and kicked off the ball. After that it was pure mayhem!

I had an opportunity to remind Bishop Brown of that many years later when, at a considerable age, he came to Rome for the Synod in 1971. He obviously did not seem to approve of me too much. I think he was always a little suspicious that perhaps I was some sort of rebel. The Irish Bishops were very conservative. One day I told him about having seen him at the football game when I was in Ireland. I mentioned how much I had appreciated the singing of "Faith of Our Fathers" and the manifestation of faith that I had witnessed at that particular time. Well, that broke down any suspicion he might have had. From then on he sought me out at the coffee breaks and always had a few words for me, asking for my opinion on the documents we had been discussing. It was a pleasant relationship and another interesting connection with my Irish roots.

***

One of the more unsettling events of our European tour was our trip to Germany. During that visit, we received some indication of things to come and what the future would hold for those who really professed their faith, particularly for any unfortunate Jewish people who were living in Germany at that time. The country was at the height of the Hitler take-over. I remember having dinner one evening at a hotel and seeing an old priest sitting alone at a table. I went over to him and asked if he would like to join Father Scott, Father Childs and myself for dinner. He was delighted.

When he joined our party, I said to him, "You know, we read a lot in the newspapers here, and in our own papers at home, and we hear a great deal about the Nazi movement, about Hitler and the question of freedom of speech in Germany. Would you object if we asked you some questions?"

"Not at all," he replied. "On the contrary, I would be very happy if you did; but let me tell you something. There are at least three Gestapo agents in this dining room. Moreover, you cannot be sure which waiters may be informers for the Gestapo. We must converse as if we are friends, just meeting. We must laugh now and then, no matter how serious the conversation becomes. Whenever a waiter comes near the table, we will change the subject. We will not speak about politics and we will not mention Hitler or the Nazi movement."

So, on that basis, we asked him to tell us what the real situation was in Germany. He told us that he had been in jail twice. He said that the Nazis had spies in the churches and that he was arrested once for saying, in a sermon, that Hitler was not God; and that people should not accept the doctrine of the absolute authority of any human being over others. For that he was put in jail for a month. On another occasion he was charged and jailed for criticising the Nazi party for not allowing people the freedom to practice their faith in peace.

He also told us that the first time he was in jail, one of Hitler's highest assistants, one of his great friends at the beginning of the "putsch", had fallen into disfavour and was in the prison cell above him. One day the priest heard what he thought was the march of the guards or the Gestapo on the floor above and he heard shots. Afterwards he learned through the prison grapevine that this man had been shot - executed in his cell.

He told us then that the reality of the situation was that absolutely nothing could stop Germany, short of a war. Hitler would not be satisfied with conquering all of Europe but would try to dominate the rest of the world as well. That priest was probably in his sixties at the time. He was very intelligent and sounded like a holy priest, and we had no difficulty in believing what he was telling us.

In those days there were still many people who were trying to defend Hitler. Those people condemned the Treaty of Versailles and used that to try to justify the take-over by Hitler. However, during the remainder of our stay in Germany, we experienced firsthand some evidence of the reality of Hitler's message.

One day we were having lunch in the hotel and some members of the Hitler Youth came in. They went from table to table and everyone was shelling out money to them. We decided we were not going to give any money to their cause, so we said "Nein." The young fellow was so absolutely unbe-

Memoirs

lieving that he just stood there with his mouth open and then finally moved away. A little later a man in uniform came into the dining room and stood watching our table. Then another man in plain clothes came in and also surveyed us. Finally they approached to just within hearing distance and when they heard us speaking English, they left. There was no doubt at all that they wanted to find out if we were Germans who had refused to contribute to the Hitler Youth. That would have been a mark against us, to say the least.

Another time, as I was leaving the hotel, I noticed a young American lady standing near the entrance. A group of men looking very drab and miserable were being marched through the streets surrounded by the Nazi guard. The lady said, "Look at those Jews. They must be going to a concentration camp." - and she took a picture. Within a minute, a Brownshirt went up to her, took the camera from her, ripped the film out of the camera and said that they were not going to a concentration camp; they were volunteers for the Army. (Such a ridiculous statement! How could those poor old people have volunteered for any Army!) Then he told her not to take any more pictures of people and said, "Stick to the scenery if you want to take pictures in Germany. We do not want you going around taking pictures and spreading propaganda against our government."

I have never been so distressed in my life to see the fear, naked fear, in the eyes of so many people. I had never experienced anything like it before and I hope I never experience anything like it again. I still look back on those days with horror and dismay.

***

By the spring of 1939, it was not too difficult to see that there was going to be a war. My friends and I had originally planned to go back to Scotland, through England once more, and to sail home around the end of August on the Cunard Line. It looked as though we were going to take the Athenia. However, the newspapers were discussing the German battleship that was going to visit Gdansk, so I became somewhat alarmed. I had a feeling that war was imminent. If that were the case, I wondered whether or not Italy would join forces with Germany right away and, if so, I certainly had no desire to be interned in Italy for the rest of the war. I suggested to Scotty and George that we would be wiser to go to France, to Cherbourg, and to return home on the Queen Mary. We decided to take just one other little side trip and return home earlier than originally planned. As it happened, war was declared at just about the time that we sailed into New York harbour. The Athenia, on which we had initially planned to sail, was sunk by the Germans. It was the first passenger boat to be torpedoed in the North Atlantic. That was in late August. It is almost certain that we would have been on that boat if we had not felt that there was going to be an outbreak of war. As events proved, we had made a very wise decision, which resulted in our safe return home.

Experiences of a Young Priest

On my arrival in New York, Emmett was there to meet me. The two of us spent several days taking in the World's Fair which was as usual a great event. I must confess, it was with a certain amount of satisfaction and joy that I finally found myself at home, back in my own surroundings, as we drove into Montreal. I naturally had to meet with Archbishop Gauthier, who was staying at his country home at Ste. Adèle in the Laurentians. Emmett volunteered to drive me there and the two of us had a very interesting conversation with the Archbishop. One thing that I find a little ironic now is that he said to us, "Je compte beaucoup sur vous, mes fils. Vous n'êtes pas séparatistes." (I count a lot on you my sons because you are not separatists.) His comment takes on an almost humorous note at this particular moment in Quebec's history.

What might have precipitated Archbishop Gauthier's remark was a certain fear of any new movement among the English-speaking Catholics, especially those with whom Father McShane was involved. Because of the influence McShane exercised in the English-speaking Church in Montreal, he was, albeit mistakenly, often suspected of trying to form a kind of English-speaking diocese within the Greater Montreal Diocese. Personally, I am certain that no such idea ever entered his mind. There is no doubt, however, that he worked diligently for the promotion of such causes as St. Mary's Hospital, St Patrick's Orphanage and the Dowd Memorial Home for elderly people, and anything of importance to the entire English-speaking Catholic presence in Montreal at that time. When we were in the Seminary and St. Mary's Hospital was being founded, Dr. Donald Hingston, Dr. Dunstan Grey and their friends would naturally have talked about this to Father McShane because of his influence with the other priests and the people. With the exception of some of the parish priests who were rather jealous of him, he did have a strong influence in the English-speaking Catholic organizations and on their leaders.

During our visit, Archbishop Gauthier told me that he wanted me to work at the Marriage Tribunal as an auditor, to help reduce the number of cases, some of which were too long-standing. Since I would have preferred to do some pastoral work, I suggested that I would like to help out in a parish, as well as doing my work at the Tribunal. The Archbishop did not agree. He felt that could create some difficulties, particularly if I had to be working on cases and the pastor thought I should be doing

Memoirs

something else. He had already made up his mind that he wanted me to become the Chaplain of St. Mary's Hospital and to work two or three afternoons at the Tribunal until we could get some of the cases looked after. I realized from the very beginning that this would be a tough assignment. We did not have any pastoral care departments in hospitals in those days. The priest who was hospital chaplain had to do practically everything himself, including night calls and patient follow-up. With such a full workload at the hospital, travelling downtown to work at the Tribunal would be an added strain. I accepted my assignment, however, without too much hesitation, and soon afterwards I joined forces again with Father Laurent Morin at the Tribunal.

St. Mary's had had a very humble origin, the first site being Lord Shaughnessy's home on what was then Dorchester Boulevard. It was a small hospital at that time. However, with the cooperation of the English-speaking parishes and their pastors and the campaigns that they ran, the present St. Mary's Hospital was built. We received only a relatively small amount of financial help from the Quebec government, so we had to campaign vigorously in every parish and every business among the English-speaking people of Montreal. I must say that they supported us well. St. Mary's became a very important hospital and made a significant contribution to health care in Montreal.

While at St. Mary's I occupied a patient's room on the third floor, opposite the solarium where they would put the critically ill. Once there were two men in that room. One refused to talk to me and would actually begin to curse and swear whenever I entered the room. The other was a very devout Catholic and a man of deep faith who welcomed my visits. He told me he had tried several times to talk to his roommate about spiritual values and received nothing but profanity in return. Eventually I began to wonder whether it was not an almost diabolical hatred that this man had for the Church. On one occasion I stopped the nurse who was taking him his dinner and I blessed his plate. He could not possibly have known that I had blessed it because we were down the hall, quite a distance from the solarium. When the nurse came out of the room, she was as white as a sheet. She told me that when she had put the plate in front of him, the man had taken his plate and, cursing and swearing, threw his whole dinner right against the wall. Days later, when I went in to annoint the Catholic man who died peacefully saying his prayers with love of the Lord, this man kept screaming his hatred of Christ. He eventually died without any sign of a change of heart. It was a very frightening and disconcerting experience which I still recall vividly. I have thought of him many times in my life and have wondered about the mystery of how God's grace touches souls.

***

I have to say that the appointment of Archbishop Joseph Charbonneau as Coadjutor with right of succession in Montreal, certainly changed my life. Charbonneau was badly received when he first arrived in Montreal in May 1940. He was given a very curt reception at the Cathedral where he was met by the Chancellor and brought to the Bishop's Residence. There the dear old porter, Theodore, took him upstairs, showed him to his room, and that was it. Shortly afterwards, during the priests' retreat, there were probably a few hundred priests or more in attendance at the Conference given by Archbishop Gauthier. Charbonneau was sitting at the back of the room. By way of introduction, Archbishop Gauthier spoke volubly in praise of the great service of his Auxiliary, Bishop Deschamps, who had shown so much loyalty to every wish and desire of the Archbishop. He said he admired Deschamps for the way he remained in the shadow of the Archbishop, never acting on his own initiative, but consulting him in all things. He ended by saying, "I hope that the one they have sent me as Coadjutor will do the same."

It was really a shocking experience. I must say immediately that Archbishop Gauthier was very ill at the time. I do not think that in his better days he would have been so lacking in charity or politeness, because he was not inclined that way. He was, however, always very stern, a little gruff, and very firm in his opinions. He was a great orator - probably one of the great French-Canadian speakers of his time. I have always felt very close to him in a certain way. I did not see him a great deal, but when I did, he was always most considerate and, as I said, he seemed to sense that we were loyal to him. He was always very open to my brother Emmett's requests concerning the English-speaking Catholic school system in Montreal. We had no Normal School, no teachers' training college. After high school, those who wanted to teach had to pass an examination and became teachers. Through Archbishop Gauthier and the power he wielded in the Catholic community, an English-speaking Normal School was begun in 1939 and later evolved into St. Joseph's Teachers' College.

I had met Charbonneau before the retreat. I admired his personality, his ability, his wisdom and especially his broad-mindedness. It seemed only right that the English-speaking priests should welcome him, so after dinner I suggested to them that we meet Archbishop Charbonneau. When he came upstairs, I introduced him to them. We welcomed him, told him how happy we were to have him as the Coadjutor Archbishop of Montreal and we moved on towards the chapel. It was very simple and informal, but I hope it may have made up a little for the rather cool reception that was given him earlier.

After Archbishop Gauthier's death in August 1940, Charbonneau took over the direction of Montreal. One of his first acts was to ask Rome to name an English-speaking Auxiliary Bishop and Father Lawrence Whelan was appointed during the summer of 1941. Emmett and I learned of the news in Nova Scotia while we were on a trip together with Fathers Scott and Childs. It had been

Memoirs

announced over the radio that Montreal had two new Bishops and one of them, Bishop Whelan, was English-speaking. This was a very courageous move on the part of Archbishop Charbonneau. The general feeling of the Suffragan Bishops of the Archdiocese of Montreal was that it was not necessary to appoint an English-speaking Auxiliary because the English-speaking Catholics were already adequately represented in the Chancery Office and they were well served.

After Bishop Whelan's appointment, I was called in by Archbishop Charbonneau and told that he would like me to take on the task of Vice-Chancellor of the Diocese while continuing as Vice-Officialis of the Tribunal. Canon Robert Mitchell was the Chancellor and a French-Canadian, though his name would suggest he was English-speaking. He and I became good friends. (Much to my regret, he became very ill in the early fifties and never really recovered.) This was certainly a more difficult assignment than I would have chosen because it meant going to the Chancery Office every day from nine to four, Monday to Friday. I was supposed to take Thursdays off. Instead I taught three classes to the nurses in the Nursing School at St. Mary's, so mine was a seven-day week. I found this rather demanding, but in those days you did not ask why or wherefore. You just went ahead and tried to carry out whatever duties were assigned to you.

One of the great inconveniences, of course, was that we were wearing soutanes with long black coats over them. This made it difficult to get on and off the streetcar every day. Fortunately, I had a friend who lived close to the hospital. Since he worked downtown, he offered to drive me to the Chancery Office each morning. Most afternoons I would take the streetcar back to the hospital where I would begin my rounds.

During those years, I was also asked by Father Jean-Paul Laurence, a Sulpician and the Superior of the Seminary of Philosophy (he later became the provincial of St. Sulpice) if I would give a class to the English-speaking students twice a week in Apologetics, particularly for the benefit of the American students who had come in fairly large numbers. It was almost ridiculous to accept, but I did. I decided I would leave the Chancery Office at four o'clock and go to the House of Philosophy and give those lads a forty-five to sixty minute class because I knew how much it would mean to them. Their knowledge of French was so limited that it gave them a little break to have a class in English. It also gave me the chance to give them the baseball and hockey scores. In those days students were not permitted to have newspapers or radios in the Seminary. Because of this I was always awaited with a certain amount of eagerness by the philosophers. We had a very good, friendly and, I think, profitable relationship. I heard from many of them later on. Some of those who persevered and went through the Seminary either in Montreal or elsewhere, would drop me a note around Christmastime to say how much they had appreciated my lectures. Teaching that class had been a very pleasant duty.

In addition to these various assignments, I received a call from the new owner and manager of the CJAD radio station in Montreal. He asked me if I would be willing to conduct a new Sunday program to be called "The Catholic Hour". Despite the fact that I already had Mass and other duties at the hospital on Sundays, I accepted because I thought it was becoming necessary for the Church to broaden its means of communication. Radio, later followed by television, did not have the same power it enjoys today, but it was exercising an increasingly greater influence in forming public opinion. The "Catholic Hour" was a new beginning for us. It was the breaking of the ice because as yet there was very little in the way of religious programming. I was able to arrange programs with my brother Emmett and other priests and with such people as Robert Keyserlingk and Murray Ballantyne, both noted Catholic journalists.

I was drawn into yet another enterprise at about that time. Bishop John Cody, of London, Ontario, had convinced the English-speaking Catholic Bishops to found a national Catholic newspaper. It was our hope that the *Ensign*, as it was christened, would unite Catholics in the various provinces throughout the country. It was a valiant venture. Our efforts to form an amalgamation with the *Catholic Register* were blocked in the beginning by Cardinal James McGuigan, Archbishop of

Toronto, who did not want to see the *Register* disappear. Despite this difficulty, we planned to proceed with the *Ensign*. Bob Keyserlingk and I met in my office at St. Mary's to look over different possibilities and to try to decide how best to use the money which the Bishops were willing to provide for this endeavour. Then I received a phone call from Cardinal McGuigan, telling me that he was willing to combine the *Register* with the *Ensign* after all. This meant, of course, that we had to change our plans and postpone the printing because new arrangements had to be initiated in order to get the *Ensign* properly organized into one national Catholic paper.

I am sorry to say that, although it fulfilled a very good purpose, and I think, did some good things, the *Ensign* never really received the full support of Toronto. The expenses continued to mount and the Bishops became reluctant to continually raise more money for the paper. Though we partially succeeded in trying to bring the country together, we also learned that Canada is very large and complicated. Coast to coast coverage proved to be extremely difficult. It was an enterprise which was probably too ambitious and never really succeeded in the way we had hoped.

I must add that Archbishop Charbonneau always showed support for the *Ensign*. Right to the very end, when the English-speaking Bishops gave up their financial support, Charbonneau was willing to pay his share. I know this from personal experience because he had named me as his representative on the Board of the *Ensign*. I attended every meeting. Having seen all the financial statements I knew why we were getting deeper and deeper into debt. Yet whenever I spoke to the Archbishop after a meeting, at no time did he say, "Oh this is too much", or "We cannot continue". He gave not only vocal but monetary support as well. He remained very interested in what we were doing and gave us great encouragement. It certainly was his desire that this national Catholic paper would grow and succeed.

One of the good things about the *Ensign* was that Bob Keyserlingk had connections with all of the news agencies. As a result, he had firsthand knowledge of news events as they were happening. For instance, our paper was one of the first to be informed that Igor Gouzenko was trying to defect and leave the Russian Embassy in Ottawa but was not having very much success in convincing anyone to take him seriously. The large daily papers would not accept the story so the *Ensign* published it. There was quite a reaction to this in some circles.

I will leave further comment on the history of the *Ensign* to those who had a more intimate knowledge of it. Only those who were working on a full-time basis at the task of turning out each issue of the paper could ever do the whole story justice. I suggest that this would certainly be an interesting thesis sometime for a student in a University, studying for a degree. It would reveal many differences of opinion and different approaches to the way of evangelizing, the way of teaching, and the way of bringing the Word of God and of the Church to our people.

***

While the *Ensign* was being published, I was talked into running a weekly column entitled "The Question Box". I must say that I am exceedingly embarrassed when I reread it now from the vantage point of years and years of experience. I come through, I am afraid, as an inexperienced know-it-all. Today I would give some considerably different answers from those I gave at the time I was writing that column. However, even though it was very elementary, perhaps it served a purpose. In those days people were looking for answers and resources were limited. Hopefully the service we tried to render, though not of earth-shaking importance, had some significance for the people whose needs we were attempting to meet.

***

I had appreciated Archbishop Charbonneau's support for the *Ensign*. He was a remarkable man in so many ways. He took very seriously the teaching of the Church on Catholic Action and encouraged the work of evangelization in Montreal. Charbonneau was also active in Social Justice, which brought him into conflict with Maurice Duplessis who had been re-elected Premier of

Memoirs

Quebec in 1944. They differed very much in their views on the rights of unions and union activity. Anyone who knows anything about that time will remember the famous Asbestos strike in 1949 and the brutality used against the striking workers. Such well-known figures as Trudeau, Pelletier, Marchand, André Laurendeau and Claude Ryan, gave their support to the workers. They were all to become leaders in the "Revolution Tranquille" (Quiet Revolution), which was just beginning to take place in Quebec. The unions were not the strong multinational corporations that they are today and could not help to support the striking members. The workers themselves had remained relatively poor because their salaries had not kept up with the prosperity which the war had started to bring into our country and into Quebec in particular.

Archbishop Charbonneau had collections taken in all of his churches to aid the striking workers who were impoverished and whose wives and children were hungry. He was criticized for this action, which today would be accepted without any hesitation. It would be normal for Church representatives to express their support for what was definitely a just cause. There is no question at all that Charbonneau was on the side of the angels in this controversy.

Duplessis had brought out a Bill, which was aimed against unionism and was out to defeat the labour unions. During a Mass Charbonneau was celebrating in Notre Dame Church, the largest church in Montreal, he denounced the Bill that had been presented to Parliament. When he came into the sacristy after Mass, his secretary, Father Paul Touchette, said to him, (Father Touchette himself told me this), "Did you realize that there were two microphones; one for the Church and one for the radio stations to broadcast your sermon all over Montreal?"

Charbonneau was very surprised, if not shocked, to hear of this. After a moment or two he said, "It is just as well. I believe in the stand I took. I believe that I am right and therefore I should have no objection to my talk being broadcast."

Some of the finest words on Catholic Action, the great cause of Pope Pius XI, have been written by Charbonneau. His letters concerning Les Jocistes (the Young Christian Workers) and Les Jécistes (the Young Christian Students) for example, certainly made a great impact in Montreal. I remember some of the meetings. Bishop Laurent Morin (Father Morin then) became very active in Catholic Action and abandoned his work at the Tribunal to give this his full attention. It was not Catholic Action as we knew it. In fact, it was the beginning of a new enterprise in the Church, Catholic Social Action. The movement brought some very fine people to the fore at a time when lay people had not really been called upon too often to play a serious and worthwhile role in the work of evangelizing society. We think of Claude Ryan and Joseph Lapierre.

Memoirs

Curiously, Ryan became a great leader in the French sector and Lapierre became a great leader in the English sector. This shows that, in Quebec, one's name is not always indicative of one's nationality. These were great people. They were very devoted, those early pioneers in Catholic Action around Montreal. One has to realize that there was an awakening at that time; that the somnolent and well-satisfied society was beginning to fall apart. Those early attempts were extremely important in the life of the Church.

The young people in our English sector benefitted significantly from the organization of Sodalities, promoted by the American Jesuit, Father Daniel Lord. My brother Emmett was the man who formed the MISSA - Montreal Inter-School Sodality Association. Daniel Lord came to Montreal several times. I was not directly involved, but I liked to accompany the students and young people in the Sodality movement to their annual assembly in New York. It was held at Fordham University by Father Lord and his well-trained and personable associates.

Those were good years and there was a lot of good work done which should not be forgotten. These associations had a great importance. They certainly had a lot of influence on some of the later leaders of society. Claude Ryan, for instance, has long been a great Christian voice in the Province of Quebec and on the political scene. Probably his best days were when he was the editor of *Le Devoir*.

It is not surprising that Charbonneau had so much interest in Catholic Action and that he would respond so fully to the wishes of the Holy Father. Indeed, it suited his personality and his ecclesiology. I still maintain that Charbonneau understood the reality of collegiality in the Church in a very special way, even before Vatican II; before all the theologians and the profoundly convinced Bishops came forward during the Council on that particular subject.

One day I went into Charbonneau's office. I had some documents that had to be signed in the Chancery Office and he said, "Sit down, I want to talk to you. Has Archbishop Murray been speaking to you?"

I replied, "No. I have not seen him. Is he in Montreal?

"Yes. He came to see me," he said. "I may as well tell you the story now that I have started. You know that Archbishop Sinnott has not been well and as a result Rome has named Archbishop Murray Administrator of the Archdiocese of Winnipeg. He has come to me with some very difficult problems. Archbishop Sinnott is reluctant to give up his authority. The Chancellor is planning to leave and the whole Diocesan situation is muddled and confused. Archbishop Murray has asked me if I would give you permission to go to Winnipeg for a few months to help out. He wants you to train one of his priests to become Chancellor because he has

Memoirs

no one at the present time who would be able to fulfill that role. He has a young priest in mind and he would like you to prepare him. Would you be willing to leave and go to Winnipeg for awhile?"

"You do not even have to ask," I said. "If you want me to go, I will go. "

This was his answer: "Father Carter, if the Church in Montreal would render this service to the Church in Winnipeg, I think it would bring a blessing to the Church of Montreal."

Those words were spoken in 1946. It was long before the debate on collegiality and the role and responsibility of the Bishop for the Universal Church. (I remembered his words later during the debate on the Church and Collegiality at the Council and I said to myself, "The ghost of Charbonneau is walking up and down that middle aisle of St. Peter's right now.") Charbonneau probably would have died the Archbishop of Montreal if he had not been a man ahead of his time.

***

Just before I was due to leave for Winnipeg, my father died. I remember the night very well. I had planned to go away for the weekend. Monseigneur Charles Valois, the Vicar-General, Canon Robert Mitchell, the Chancellor in Montreal, and I were going to do some trout fishing and they were to call for me on Friday night. I had seen Dad that evening and I did not like the look of him so I decided not to make the trip. When Valois and Mitchell drove to St. Mary's Hospital to pick me up, I told them I could not leave because it seemed to me that Dad's condition was beginning to deteriorate.

When I returned to my father, he asked, "What are you doing here?"

I simply said, "Our trip has been postponed."

I went over on Saturday and annointed him on his death bed with some of the family gathered around and at about two o'clock Sunday morning, Dad died.

As we knelt together at the bedside, I remember saying to Mother and my sister Margaret, "Let's say a prayer to thank the Lord for having taken Dad out of his misery and pain. He has enjoyed his life. He would have been very unhappy as a bedridden patient, so let us be grateful to God for His grace and His blessing."

Emmett was living at the Normal School in those days and there was no way of getting in touch with him at that hour. As soon as I could reach him Sunday morning, he came home. We made all of the arrangements for the funeral and the Mass was celebrated at St. Patrick's. I was very fond of my father and his death was a great loss in my life.

After the funeral, I contacted Archbishop Murray and asked him if it was possible for me to wait until September to go to Winnipeg. We were now into June and I wanted to stay at home for awhile. The family needed to be together to support one another and to support our mother. Archbishop Murray had no objection.

***

I arrived in Winnipeg in September. I learned in more detail the facts surrounding their current situation and was given a brief history of the Diocese of Winnipeg. Archbishop Alfred Sinnott had been a very bright man, but in his later years he had deteriorated mentally. The treatment he gave Archbishop Gerald Murray was indicative of the way that he had lost touch. When Archbishop Murray arrived as Coadjutor, he was badly received. He was not invited to stay at St. Mary's, the Cathedral Parish. Instead, he was sent off to the Jesuit Parish of St. Ignatius where, thankfully, he was very warmly welcomed and where they were delighted to have him. He was asked to do some Confirmations but every now and then he would get a phone call as he was about to leave, only to be told not to bother going because the Archbishop would go himself. This was the kind of life Murray had as a Coadjutor. I urged him to put some pressure on Rome to clear up the situation, but he would just smile and shrug and say that he was not going to bother.

Shortly after my arrival, I wrote to Archbishop Charbonneau. I told him that I would have to stay in Winnipeg for a year, or nine months at least, because so much work had to be done. I could see that the whole undertaking would certainly require more time than had been allotted. The Archbishop wrote back and said, "Fine. If that is the situation, please clear it up for Archbishop Murray and help him all you can."

Father Maurice Cooney was the priest I was to introduce into Chancery work. He was a very fine man and a good companion. I enjoyed working with him, but I found the task challenging. Among other things, the major document on "Preparation for Marriages", which had been in effect in other dioceses in Canada for several years, had not even been issued in Winnipeg. I had to issue it, prepare new questionnaires, translate them into French and then send them around to the parishes. There were also serious financial problems in the Diocese. Collections were relatively small. There were expired debentures bringing in no interest. I had to take those debentures and return them immediately, investing the money in interest-bearing bonds to help us meet our expenses.

Archbishop Murray and I certainly had a few adventures together. Archbishop Sinnott maintained that he was still the head of the Corporation and he named, as Chancellor, one of the older priests who was afraid to argue with him or question him. He sent his own personal seal to be repaired and also ordered the seal of the Corporation. Fortunately, the company telephoned me and asked if they could deliver Archbishop Sinnot's seals to St. Mary's because it would cost a few dollars to send them to Camp Morton where he was then living. I asked which seals they were talking about and they told me. I said, "You can bring them to the Cathedral if you wish, and we will look after them."

At that time, Archbishop Murray was in Ottawa. I telephoned him to let him know what was happening and I said, "Now that you are in Ottawa, you had better see the Apostolic Delegate and have this matter settled once and for all. If Archbishop Sinnott gets possession of the Corporation seal, it is going to complicate things because he is talking about borrowing $100,000.00. I have had to go to the managers of the banks in Winnipeg and instruct them not to lend him any money. So it is imperative that this situation be straightened out in Rome right away."

Murray said he would think about it. But, he did not do anything. In the meantime, I wrote to Archbishop Sinnott and told him that the seals had arrived. He would drop in occasionally to see the housekeeper at St. Mary's and have a little chat, but he never came to see the Archbishop or myself. I informed him that I was leaving his personal seal with the housekeeper so he could pick it up anytime he wished. "But," I continued, "I am afraid I cannot let you have the Corporation seal because obviously it has to be kept here. Archbishop Murray is now responsible for the finances and all diocesan affairs because he is the Administrator."

It was not long before I received Archbishop Sinnott's reply. He was very gentle when you met him, but when he wrote you a letter, he could be very aggressive. Sinnott told me that he was going to sue me in the Civil Court and bring charges against me to the Sacred Congregation of the Consistorial, which is now the Congregation of Bishops in Rome. He said that if I kept the Corporation seal, he would keep ordering more until he finally got one. Then he ended his letter with, "Bowing to your superior knowledge" or words to that effect.

I had to telephone the company that made the seals and explain the situation to the best of my ability. I said, "Archbishop Sinnott is probably going to order another seal, and we are asking you not to make one. That seal is a Corporation seal and Archbishop Murray is the Administrator of the Corporation. There is no way that he can allow this."

They said, "How can we refuse him a seal if he asks for one?"

I replied, "Would you make a seal for the Royal Bank at the request of someone who was not the manager of the Royal Bank? Then do not do it for the Corporation of the Archdiocese of Winnipeg either. Archbishop Sinnott, though he still has a title, is effectively retired. If he borrows money in the name of the Corporation because you have given him an official seal which we have asked you not to give him, I think you might find yourselves liable to be sued."

That being the case they agreed to ignore any further request for a seal.

I then got in touch with Archbishop Sinnott and said, "Look, this is a legal question. You cannot possibly claim that you are the head of the Corporation when you do not have the power of administration."

"Well," he said, "if you can get a legal opinion for me from Pitblado or Williams, I will accept it."

Mr. E.K. Williams was an Anglican, and a truly great gentleman who later became a judge. As an example of his courtesy: when I telephoned him to say that Archbishop Murray would like to visit with him, and asked when we could go to his office, he said, "If the Archbishop wants to see me I will go to his office."

When Williams came, we gave him the letters from Rome and the legal document setting up the Corporation of the Archdiocese of Winnipeg. He took it under consideration and in two or three days wrote back saying that there was no question at all. Archbishop Murray was undoubtedly the Administrator and was the official head of the Corporation by the very fact that he had been appointed Administrator. There was no doubt, then, that he had the power to control the spiritual and temporal affairs of the Archdiocese.

We immediately sent a copy of this letter to Archbishop Sinnott who refused to accept the decision of the very lawyer he had recommended. Sinnott still felt he had the right to run the affairs of the Archdiocese. It was a ticklish situation. Strangely enough, it continued until Archbishop Philip Pocock, who had been Bishop of Saskatoon since 1944, succeeded Murray as Coadjutor in 1951. He brought the matter to a head by giving an ultimatum to Cardinal Piazza, who was then the head of the Congregation of the Consistorial, and who had come to Canada on a visit. Pocock warned that if they did not clear this matter up once and for all and make him the Archbishop of Winnipeg, there would be another Bishop retired in Victoria.

My most rewarding time in Winnipeg was that spent with Archbishop Murray. I have met many priests in my life; I have met many bishops and many leading Catholics, but I have rarely met a man like Archbishop Gerald Murray, who seemed to me to be a living saint, a man of great patience. He was so humble, so tolerant. He was a bishop of the old school undoubtedly. He had an immense amount of understanding and sympathy for the priests. Working with him was a delight. Every morning I went to the Convent of the Sisters of Service for Mass at six-thirty. Then I usually worked until about nine o'clock at night, if I was not with the Archbishop on Confirmation tours or out on other business. Most of the time we were at home in the late evening. Each night I would hear the shuffle of the Archbishop's slippers as he came from his room towards mine, which was at the other end of the hall. Perhaps the greatest compliment I could pay him - in fact anybody - is that I never once felt that I would rather not have seen him come for the CBC night news on the radio. We would sit and listen to the news together and then we would talk about old times in Montreal where Archbishop Murray had spent time when he was Provincial of the Redemptorist Fathers. That hour I spent with him at night was always a very precious time, and we never once ran out of things to talk about. It was a warm experience and I learned a great deal from him. Unfortunately I did not have the character or the virtue to live up to his own basic kindness and breadth of understanding, but at least I do think that this man had a very salutary influence on me.

I must say too that I admired the priests of Winnipeg. Their situation, even in the schools, was very difficult - so different from what I was used to in Montreal - and certainly different from what we are used to now in Ontario. For instance, there was a Catholic elementary school across from the Cathedral and not only did they have to pay taxes on the land, but on the building as well. They received no aid at all from the government. Out of its own revenues, the Cathedral Parish had to pay for all repairs and renovations and also the nominal salaries of the dedicated Sisters from Montreal. Since this was a missionary work, the Sisters accepted a minimal salary and yet they worked very hard to help the children. I do not know how many Western Catholics realize or remember the immense contribution that the French-Canadian Sisters made in the early days of the West. Western hospitals and schools would not have existed without the Sisters of St. Anne, the Sisters of the Holy Name, and the Sisters of Jesus and Mary. That is a great part of our history that should not be forgotten and which some day should be completely written.

I was touched by the fact that before I left, the priests of Winnipeg held a going away celebration for me at the hotel. They were profuse in their thanks and appreciation. I was very moved by this because I knew that they had been wary of me when I first arrived. Being Westerners, they were very frank when I suggested that their attitude toward me had changed.

As we chatted I said to them, "When I arrived in Winnipeg I knew right away I was not welcome, but after awhile I had the feeling that we were beginning to get along very well. But, you know, this farewell gesture is the crowning of it all. I am so grateful that in one year we were able to develop this kind of friendship."

They said, "Yes. At first we thought, 'Here comes a big-shot Montrealer - a big Canon lawyer - coming out to tell us poor Westerners, us poor farmers, how we should be running the Church and what we should be doing.' Then when we met you, you did not try to throw your weight around at all. We gradually came to appreciate very much the fact that what you were doing was helping us to do our job." So, their spokesman, known affectionately as the Gloomy Dean, told me that they were determined not to let me go without a good, congenial and fraternal party.

When I went back for a meeting in Winnipeg as President of the Canadian Conference of Bishops in the late sixties, many of those same priests came up and renewed acquaintance. It was very fulfilling for me. I have never regretted the experience of that year. In fact, I think that it probably had an influence on my life because I experienced the Western spirit and the Western consciousness of their own growing importance in this country and in the Church.

***

Once my assignment in Winnipeg was completed, and before I returned home, my brother Emmett and our old friend Father Walter Sutton joined me there and we travelled to the west coast for a holiday. We went as far as Victoria and then returned home to Montreal in August. Emmett was going to make a thirty-day retreat. I had to telephone him a few days before the retreat to let him know that our older brother Tom had died of a heart attack in Atlantic City where he was living at the time. He and his wife, Ilona, who was four months pregnant, had gone to the beach. Tom spotted a young girl who, having gone out too far, was caught in a strong ocean current and was in danger of drowning. He dove in and helped to rescue her.

Just as they were approaching the beach and were in knee-deep water, Tom turned to one of the lifeguards involved in the rescue attempt and gasped, "Get me ashore." The lifeguards brought him to dry land where he collapsed in the sand. Tom was rushed to hospital where he died shortly after. Five months later Ilona gave birth to their daughter Michele. Now two deaths had occurred in our family; Dad's had preceded my trip to Winnipeg and my brother Tom's had concluded it.

***

Upon my return to Montreal, Archbishop Charbonneau asked me if I would like to live at the Cathedral and intimated that he wanted me to become a Canon of the Chapter. I told him very frankly that I just could not visualize myself working in an office with only that to do. I would prefer to go back to my ministry in the hospital and continue part-time work in Administration, but not in the Chancery Office because by then Father Theodore Mooney was the English-speaking Chancellor, and there was no need for my services. I said that I would be delighted simply to go back to work on the Tribunal with Bishop Valérien Bélanger (and then later with Father Leonard Crowley who joined us). The Archbishop very willingly honoured my request and I prepared to resume these familiar duties - but under quite different circumstances, as I would soon discover.

Carter in his youth.

The Carter brothers: Emmett, Cyril, Tom and Alex.

A student of Canon Law in Rome, 1937-1939.

Celebration of the 50th Wedding Anniversary of Tom and Mary Carter, 1945.

Ordained a priest in Montreal, June 6, 1936.

With Cardinal Paul-Emile Léger.

Carter stands next to Pope Pius XII during a 1954 audience.

Two of Carter's sisters, Mother Mary Lenore and Mother Mary Carter.

Consecrated Bishop in Notre Dame Basilica, Montreal, February 2, 1957.

At the sessions of Vatican II, 1962-1965.

Alex and Emmett Carter at the Vatican II Council in Rome.

With Cardinal Leo Suenens.

Challenged!

What I came back to in Montreal was a growing tension - tension between Premier Maurice Duplessis and Archbishop Charbonneau and also tension between Charbonneau and some of the Bishops of Quebec. One of the first bones of contention was the permission the Archbishop gave to priests to wear suits - black suits and Roman collars - on the streets of Montreal. This came about because some of the English-speaking priests were voicing much resentment about having to wear soutanes winter and summer. I was then in the Chancery Office and they asked if I would arrange for them to have a meeting with the Archbishop where this could be discussed. To that end a committee was named. As I recall, the members of that committee were Monsignor McDonagh, who was a parish priest in Westmount, Father Koster, the Redemptorist pastor at that time at St. Anne's and Father Gerald Berry, who was then in charge of Catholic Charities in Montreal and who later became the Bishop of Peterborough and eventually the Archbishop of Halifax. I was to accompany these priests to the meeting. We met with Archbishop Charbonneau and he was quite sympathetic. He had come from Ottawa where the English-speaking priests already wore suits while the French-speaking priests still preferred to wear soutanes. It was simply a matter of choice.

"But," said Charbonneau, "I do not know where I stand canonically, because in Ottawa there were some arguments when the English-speaking priests started wearing suits. I heard the Council of Quebec quoted as saying that where the soutane was being worn, it should continue to be worn."

I said, "I do not think that the Council of Quebec would have the right to interfere with the local Ordinary's authority on such a question as dress. But, do you want me to study the question for you?"

"Yes," he answered. "Please prepare a canonical paper on it."

I had worked on Canon Law and the rights of local Ordinaries, and I was also familiar with the Plenary Council of Quebec. I came to the conclusion that the Archbishop had the right, within the General Code, of course, to make the change in the regulation concerning clerical dress.

Then I saw in the book by Chelodi, an expert in Canon Law, a note at the bottom of a page referring to a Roman document which had been sent to Archbishop Francis McNally of Halifax on the question of clerical attire. I wrote for a copy of the document and sure enough, there it was. Clearly, the Archbishop had the right to opt for, or let his priests opt for, the clerical dress of suit and Roman collar. He was not bound to follow the decree of the Council of Quebec. So much for the canonical right. Now, of course, came the question - was the change advisable? The Archbishop naturally had done some consulting and he had received very differing opinions. There was strong opposition to the change from some of the Bishops of Quebec. That I know.

I remember taking a walk one night in St. Agathe with my brother Emmett, Archbishop Charbonneau and our friend Murray Ballantyne. It was about twenty degrees below zero, and as we walked the mile to and from John's Lake, the Archbishop came and took my arm for a moment and said, "By the way, I have made up my mind. I am going to grant permission to any priest who wants it. I am not going to make any distinction between French and English." (Again, you see, a sign of wisdom.) "Those who so wish can wear a suit and Roman collar and they are not obliged to wear the soutane in public."

Naturally there was jubilation on the part of many of us - and not just the English-speaking priests. I am sure some of the French-speaking priests were also glad, although most of them, in those days, were not very enthusiastic. Many were brought up in small villages and parishes and they did not take to the change amiably. I know that this was the beginning of a rift between the Archbishop of Montreal and some of the Bishops of the dioceses around Montreal. It was the beginning of the end actually. But it was only the beginning. That alone could not have brought about the frightful and frightening developments that happened in the Church of Montreal.

Other moves that Charbonneau made deepened the rift between him and his associates. I remember one specific incident which occurred while on a clergy retreat. The suburban Bishops had come in for the retreat as they always did. The staff of the Cathedral were also making the retreat, and at the invitation of the Archbishop, I moved into the Cathedral for that week and took part in the retreat. One night, when most of the staff had left, we were standing around chatting when, all of a sudden, Archbishop Charbonneau wondered out loud. (The Archbishop, who liked an argument, used to throw out suggestions or ask for opinions.) He wondered whether, since they had Catholic and Protestant School Boards in Montreal, there should not be a school board for the Jewish people also.

He remarked, "After all, why should the Jewish students have to be educated under the auspices of the Protestant School Board when they have their own religion? They believe in God, and they have their own faith. Should we not be broad-minded enough to consider the possibility of setting up a special board for the education of the Jewish children under a Jewish school commission?"

I have rarely seen men so angry. They objected vehemently. They could not even contemplate the possibility! Now to be fair, we have to go back to a very different age with different customs and different attitudes.

When they left, I turned to the Archbishop and said, "Did you have to do that? Don't you know that so many of the things you are doing are already being called into question by these men? Are you going out of your way to antagonize them?"

"No, no. I have been thinking about this for some time," he said. "I have a conviction that there is something at least to be considered here. I think it was my duty to air it. Obviously my brother Bishops are not in accord. I am not trying to convince them. I am not trying to push them into anything. But on the other hand, you have to remember that I am the Archbishop of Montreal. I am not the Bishop of St. Jean; I am not the Bishop of Valleyfield; I am not the Bishop of St. Hyacinth; I am the Archbishop of Montreal and I should be able to express an opinion or discuss with them an opinion which I think has some validity in the mixed population of our large and growing city."

"Well, I think that you should proceed slowly with some of your suggestions," I said. "Let some time elapse before you throw out too many new ideas."

Alex Carter

The third element that deepened the rift between the Archbishop and some of the people in the Church of Montreal was, I believe, his desire to start French high schools. Remember, this was long before the Quebec government's Parent Commission made its recommendations on reforming the school system. This was before the "Révolution Tranquille". Charbonneau confided in me that while he admired classical colleges, he was not satisfied that they answered all the needs of his compatriots. He said he could not content himself with seeing so many young people working as waiters, tradesmen and clerks. Surely there should be more positions of prominence available to them than the professions of doctor, lawyer or clergy.

He said, "Father Carter, we have to rectify the situation of one child out of five, ten or fifteen children families being able to attend a classical college and continue on to university. We must have an equivalent to the English Catholic high school so that all of our French-Canadian children will at least have the opportunity to go on to university. They must be as well prepared as those educated in the English Catholic school system."

Soon, he began to speak along that line and to make these statements publicly. One afternoon the Superiors of all the classical colleges in Quebec were arriving for a meeting which had been scheduled. Once again I saw Archbishop Charbonneau standing alone and isolated. I heard the vehemence with which these religious and secular priests opposed his ideas concerning high school education. They did not want the classical college system touched at all. It was part and parcel of the Quebec mentality and the Quebec picture. Without saying it exactly, they almost invited him to leave his Ontario ideas behind him and to accept the reality of the social situation and educational system in Quebec. This is not hearsay. I was present at the meeting.

Because of my position in the Chancery Office, I was in touch with a large number of people. Many priests came regularly to the Chancery Office for one reason or another, and those of us working in the Office made appointments for the Archbishop. We did most of the screening - we were the middle men - because of the large number of appointments the Archbishop of Montreal had. They would be waiting four, five and six at a time, sitting outside his door. Naturally, we were the confidants of many of the priests who came to see Archbishop Charbonneau and of many of the people around the Archbishop's residence, including the Canons of the Chapter. Now and then, one would pick up little vibes from their conversations and one of the things I detected was a growing dissatisfaction with Charbonneau. There were strange little inquiries being made - some of which were very mean. For example, they would ask, "How often does he visit the Chapel during the day?" or "How much time does he spend before the Blessed Sacrament?"

It was obvious that the opposition against him was mounting. One of the plausible excuses being used was that Archbishop Charbonneau was not a good administrator. Now, there is no doubt at all, to my mind, that he did not always pay full attention to administrative details and he was sometimes slow at answering his mail. But the real problem was that he was just too honest and too much of a man. He had respect for the position of the Archbishop. He knew that the responsibility for the Church in Montreal was his, that the leadership of that Church was his. I recall several instances when he made that very clear.

Archbishop Ildebrando Antoniutti, the Apostolic Delegate, had been a long time in Canada - too long in fact. At one time he was admitted to the Sacred Heart Hospital in Montreal for a rest and minor surgery. While there, for some reason, he decided that the hour of morning Mass should be changed and told the Mother Superior that the Sisters should get up at a different hour - I do not remember whether it was earlier or later. Archbishop Charbonneau went to the hospital to pay him a courtesy visit and just as he was leaving, the Superior asked to see him. She explained the situation to Charbonneau, saying that it would be very inconvenient for the Sisters to change their hour of rising. They had a program for the day and they had worked out a schedule which best suited the work they had to do and the prayers they had to say.

Archbishop Charbonneau replied, "You keep the schedule you have. I am the Archbishop of Montreal. It is nobody else's business. And, as the

Archbishop of Montreal, I would certainly never consider trying to interfere in the internal affairs of the Sisters. Just ignore the request."

Another incident occurred which further illustrates the respect that Charbonneau had for his Office as Archbishop. I went to see him one day on business and he said, "Alex, I want to show you something." He took out an envelope sent from Archbishop Antoniutti, opened it, and there was a page torn out of the *Semaine Religieuse*, which was the Montreal diocesan bulletin on the affairs of the local Church. It was an article stating that the Apostolic Delegate in Washington had learned that Rome had given a certain permission (I cannot recall what it was) which did not seem to be limited to any particular diocese. It was an interpretation which pleased Archbishop Charbonneau, so he took this little article which he had found and gave it to the person who was printing the *Semaine Religieuse*. The article was printed over the Archbishop's signature. He stated that he agreed with this interpretation and that this particular permission could now be considered as applying in Montreal.

In the envelope from Antoniutti was this one torn-out page and on top of it was written in heavy ink, "Only the Apostolic Delegate can interpret for Canada. The Apostolic Delegate in the United States has no authority here."

So, I said to Charbonneau, "You are not going to get excited about that are you?"

He answered, "I am not going to accept this kind of treatment; I am going to reply in kind."

So, he simply wrote at the bottom of the same page that the Apostolic Delegate should not be writing to the Archbishop of Montreal in such a manner. This shows the timbre of the man, the quality of the man. It was probably his honesty and his forthrightness, more than anything else, that did him in.

While Charbonneau was still in office, I took the liberty at one point of asking him why he did not go to see the Holy Father and explain the complexities of the Archdiocese of Montreal and why he felt obliged in conscience to make certain adjustments.

"You know," I said, "there is an underground movement against you. I think that it would be prudent and wise for you to see the Holy Father and bring him up-to-date on what is happening here. It would be unfortunate if he received a one-sided view which did not reflect the true picture of the situation in our Archdiocese."

Charbonneau looked at me and said, "You know, Father Carter, anytime the Holy See is not satisfied with my administration, I am willing to resign."

"I understand, Your Grace, and that is fine for you," I said, "but I think that you also have to think about us. Your coming brought a breath of fresh air into the lives of many of our priests. You have done a lot of things that took courage. You have made our ministry more acceptable and more effective. We would not want to see that changed, and I wish you would make it a point to consider this."

"I will think about it," was his reply. Unfortunately, he thought about it and did nothing.

Charbonneau knew he had made enemies among the Quebec politicians, and some of the Bishops of Quebec. He was aware that even some of the English-speaking Bishops in Canada did not agree with his approach. When he made his *ad limina* visit to Rome a short time later, he had expected a great deal of criticism because he knew that allegations had been brought against him. Strangely enough, one of the things he told me when he returned was that he had had a very pleasant and agreeable visit with the Holy Father. He was surprised that everyone in the Congregations received him so well and that he had been given such a charming reception. They brought up only one complaint. They said that representations had been made to the Holy Father about his bringing Polish orphans to Canada after the war. An accusation had been made that he had spent the money of the Propagation of the Faith to bring these orphans over. Charbonneau hastened to assure them that this was not true; that when the Chapter in Montreal had refused to approve the funds for this, he had actually spent his own money to do so. This was money that he had saved when he was Rector of the Normal School in Ottawa. He had earned a good salary and had put most of it away to be used for charitable purposes.

All in all, he was satisfied with his visit to Rome and he returned to Montreal happy, with a sense that all was well. He could not have been more wrong. Very shortly after that, within the year in fact, he was asked to resign and was told he had to leave Montreal. All those smiling faces had meant nothing.

As I recall, a few days before the final denouement of the Charbonneau affair, I happened to stay at the Cathedral one evening for supper. I was sitting next to the Archbishop and there was tension at the table that I did not understand. I noticed he was very shaky. He hardly touched his food and I could not understand what was wrong with him. I asked, "Are you alright?" and he said, "Oh yes." Then, strangely enough he started to reminisce. He talked about many of the days that we had spent together and recalled our winter holiday in St. Agathe. As he was recounting some of the experiences that we had shared, I wondered why he seemed to be in such a reminiscent mood, going back over the years. I only understood the reason for it later. Everyone was under secrecy at the time so I would not have been informed. I could sense that something was wrong, but when you have no facts you do not leap to conclusions. Post factum, as I recall that conversation, I realize why he was so upset and deeply troubled.

Shortly after that evening, I began to suspect what was happening. I had to go to Kingston with Father McShane who had some business to attend to with the Archbishop. Archbishop O'Sullivan said to me, "Well, Father Carter, how are things in Montreal?"

"They are not good at all," I answered. "To tell you the truth, they are very bad."

"Oh, you Montrealers are always complaining," he chided.

"No, it is not the usual thing. We are very worried."

Nothing more was said at the time. After dinner O'Sullivan turned to the priests and said, "I would like a few minutes with Father Carter." We went into his office and he asked, "What's wrong? Have you got some news from Montreal?"

"Yes. From all indications, it is apparent that our Archbishop is being forced out."

"Come on, I do not believe it."

"No, it is a fact and it is imminent. There is no time to lose. Actually, that is why I was going to ask to see you. I thought that you and Cardinal McGuigan might be able to do something about this and pressure Rome to put a hold on this action because obviously there is a great injustice being done here."

O'Sullivan expressed his concern, but he did not see what he could do about it, so I went home. I telephoned Archbishop Murray. Murray would not believe me at first. He said, "It can't be true, Alex.

Surely there is no way that could be done. My God, not Charbonneau!"

"Look - I am not kidding. This is going to happen and it is going to happen within a few days. I wish I had known a month earlier so I could have contacted you sooner."

"Well, what can we do?"

"I was thinking that perhaps you could get in touch with Pocock and other Bishops from the West. They could send a wire to the Holy See asking them to stop all action on the Charbonneau affair until a delegation can be sent to see the Holy Father."

"I will certainly get in touch with them," Archbishop Murray said, "and when I do I will call you back." But it was all too late. A few days later, the shock came. Charbonneau had left Montreal, flown to Victoria and moved into Mount St. Mary's Home for the Aged, in the care of the Sisters of St. Anne. He had resigned as Archbishop of Montreal.

The day after his departure, the atmosphere was very tense at the Cathedral. It was obvious that people were disturbed. I think some felt very badly. Some may even have felt that they had been indirectly responsible for what had transpired; they may have felt that they had been used. Personally, I could not believe this had happened. During that first week, I would wake up at night and think I had dreamt it. It was only after I was awake for awhile that I would realize it was not a dream at all; the nightmare was real.

There were many strange events surrounding Charbonneau's departure which were only brought to my attention after the Archbishop had left Montreal. During his time in office, one of the things Charbonneau had done was to respond to a request from some leading French-speaking Catholics in Montreal who wanted a different form of classical education for their children. What they were requesting was a type of *gymnase* based exactly on the education system of France, so Charbonneau opened Collège Stanislas and brought priests from France to staff it. Because the school was answering a small need, it did not fulfill the purpose for which it was intended and eventually there were not enough students to continue. One of the priests from the College, a very fine man who had received a letter from Charbonneau, told me the following story in my office at the Chancery:

A student came to see him one day and as they chatted for a moment or two he sensed that there was something bothering the youngster. Finally, the young man burst into tears.

He said, "I have done something terrible and I had to come to tell you. I stole a letter out of your desk. I stole the letter that you received from Archbishop Charbonneau."

When Father asked why he would do that, he said, "I was told that my tuition would be paid if I could get that letter and deliver it to someone in the Apostolic Delegation."

Shortly after the Archbishop left for Victoria, I received a call from a Quebec labour leader who asked if I would receive him privately. I said I certainly would.

"Do not come down to the office," I cautioned. "Come and see me at St. Mary's Hospital."

So he did. We spent about an hour together. He told me of the great worry and concern in labour circles in Quebec over the departure of Archbishop Charbonneau. They thought it might be due to his sympathy for the working people, particularly his efforts to effect a change in the Bill that Duplessis was proposing, and his aid to the strikers at the time of the Asbestos affair. He was relieved when I told him that I did not think that was the case. Premier Duplessis could not, by himself, have secured the removal of Archbishop Charbonneau. I said that the problem was far more an internal one - that Charbonneau had some enemies in the Church who had obviously built up a case against him and who undoubtedly exercised powerful influence. Had there been any intervention on the part of Duplessis, it would only have been of secondary importance. Unfortunately any such intervention could have helped to confirm Rome in its decision. They would not have been able to ignore the representations of the Premier of a strongly Catholic province like Quebec. However, I assured the man that this alone would not have been the reason for Charbonneau's forced resignation. I was afraid it went deeper into Church circles and that Charbonneau was not simply the victim of a political cabal or party, but was perhaps the sacrificial lamb in our own clerical circles in the Church in Quebec.

I have to say that he left appeased but not reconciled; and assured, at least, that it had not been simply a political manoeuvre, which would have left the unions in a state of consternation. At the time, as I have said before, they were not the powerful organizations they are today. Union members were still in a position where they had to struggle for decent wages and protection under the law.

It is hard recalling these events. They are still very painful. This sore is a running sore and it has never healed. Some subsequent events did not help either. One of Charbonneau's very good friends, Monseigneur Deschênes, who was a Vicar General in the Archdiocese of Montreal, went to visit Charbonneau in Victoria shortly after he had left Montreal. When Deschênes returned he was told he should resign from his parish. It appeared that anyone who continued their association with the Archbishop was considered a "persona non grata". He was a strong man, however, and said, "No way. If they want me to resign they had better form a tribunal and bring some accusation against me that would warrant a forced resignation."

After I was made a Bishop, my first trip was to Victoria to visit Charbonneau. That was when I finally heard the whole story. It is still stamped in my memory. He told me that he had been asked by the Delegate, Archbishop Antoniutti, to go to see him in Ottawa on the first of January. Charbonneau smiled at me and said, "At the beginning of the Holy Year, the year of mercy and forgiveness, I was called to see the Delegate."

When Charbonneau explained that he always spent New Year's Day with his family, so was unable to go on that day, Antoniutti agreed to see him the day after, on the second. On his arrival in Ottawa, Archbishop Antoniutti told him that word had come from Rome that they were dissatisfied with him and wanted his resignation. Charbonneau was taken completely by surprise.

Returning to Montreal, he asked Bishop Bélanger, an Auxiliary in Montreal, a canon lawyer and the head of the Tribunal, to prepare a defence vindicating his years as Archbishop of Montreal, explaining and defending what he had done. Bélanger was in the process of drawing up a brief when the Apostolic Delegate arrived in Montreal. Charbonneau told the Delegate he was appealing officially to the Congregation of the Consistorial and personally to the Holy Father. The Delegate told him that there was no appeal to be made because the decision was not from the Congregation. The decision was the personal decision of the Pope. The Delegate also informed him that he would have to leave within a short time, stating the number of days.

Charbonneau said to Archbishop Antoniutti, "I have served the Church as priest and Bishop loyally. You have made a decision and you tell me there is no appeal. Well, Your Grace, I suggest that when you leave here" - he was at the Cathedral Rectory on Cathedral Street - "you take your book of Canon Law with you and turn left as you go out the door. Walk right down the street until you come to the St. Lawrence River. Then I suggest that you throw it into the river. It does not mean anything if there is no appeal from such a decision, and no hearing or no right to answer whatever accusations have been made. I am not even given a chance to vindicate myself." He said, "I would not treat the least of my priests, or the worst of my priests, in such a way without hearing them out - without finding out the facts."

I think that the following letter, which I received from the Archbishop shortly after he left Montreal, speaks for itself.

Alex Carter

Mount St. Mary
Victoria, B.C.
March 14, 1950

Dear Father Carter,

With you I have been profoundly scandalized by all that came upon me in last January.

I thought first that the first step against me had been taken by the Consistorial - from their decision. I appealed to the Holy Father, I asked for a hearing. I wrote to Mgr. Montini for a private audience, I insisted to be told the reasons for my amotion etc.

But when the Apostolic Delegate summoned His Excellency Bishop Whelan and Mgr. Bélanger to Ottawa and practically told them that, not the Consistorial, but the Secretariat of State, the Holy Father himself was demanding my resignation, what could I do? - I was denied the elementary right to be heard, to defend myself, to vindicate at least my good faith - I was told the decision was irrevocable and no appeal receivable.

I presumed thus that the Vicar of Christ had reasons to act that way against me and I resigned my See. Later on I first learned by a Victoria paper that I had been transferred to the Titular See of Bosphorus.

Now to tell you the truth, I could not recognize our Mother the Church in all that befell me - at the beginning of the Holy Year, a period of general absolution.

Memoirs

As a student and a professor of Canon Law, I had been led to admire the spirit of Justice and equity that pervades our code. As a bishop I was refused the protection of that law. I was condemned and was not given an opportunity to defend myself.

I always thought that we could rely on Church authorities to be treated in a gentleman's way - I was dealt with sternly, brutally, without any regard either for my person or for my functions.

This apparent lack of justice, charity and courtesy has dazzled me, has stunned me.

You remember the story of that good nun who had been appointed by her Superior as door-keeper of her convent and was recommended never to refuse to give alms to those in need coming to the house for charity. "We never know, it may be Our Lord, or St. Joseph who comes that way in the disguise of the poor." "Believe me, when you did it to one of the least of my brethren here, you did it to me." - we read in S. Matthew.

But still one day, the good religious came across a man half-drunk, smelling of liquors - what was she going to do! The man in her presence certainly was not Our Lord - or St. Joseph - was she so terribly wrong to react in that way?

Like the good nun, in my trial, I could not first recognize the loving face of Mother Church - I obeyed, but my heart was broken and my mind abashed -

Alex Carter

To comply with the desires of the Apostolic Delegate I hurried to leave Montreal and on the 31st of January I flew to Victoria.

More than a month has elapsed now. I become more and more reconciled to my new situation. I am free of all responsibility, I sleep better, I was welcomed by very kind Sisters and received by a very sympathetic bishop.

Of course, I miss you all bitterly. I suffer much by a certain isolation in ideas and feelings, chiefly by being so far away from all those who are dear to me - the will of God be done!

From the start I have forgiven all to all - it is not so easy to forget.

A friend of mine has hinted that the blow had been dealt from Rimouski. I don't mind much now - provided I find some opportunity to continue to serve my Good Lord and to save the souls He has redeemed - There is one thing I wish to adhere to to the last: your sympathy and your friendship.

Totus tibi in Christo
+J. Charbonneau

I am well aware that my admiration for Archbishop Charbonneau, our close friendship and his kindness to me personally is perhaps a factor in the horror that I still feel when I review this. I look back on those years, and I remember so many pleasant things. I used to prepare some of his speeches for him because he had so many places to go and so many things to do. Sometimes he would come to the hospital on a Sunday, sit down in my office, have a cigarette and say, "Oh Father Carter, would you do me a favour?" And I would say without hesitation, "How can I help you?"

Seeing a man who was so obviously at the peak of his service to the Church and doing so much good in Montreal suddenly cut off and practically exiled, it is no wonder that, to this day and even in my old age, I still resent the injustice that was perpetrated.

If anyone were to ask me what experience I had as a priest that shocked me the most, I would have to say it was the treatment given to Archbishop Charbonneau. It was one of the greatest miscarriages of justice that I have ever known in the Church, and I personally have never been reconciled to it.

So ends the story as I lived it and shared in it. I let the curtain fall on the Charbonneau affair.

***

Naturally there was great concern and interest among the clergy in Montreal as to who would succeed Archbishop Charbonneau. Some of us thought it might well be the Rector of the Canadian College, Monseigneur Paul-Emile Léger, who had distinguished himself in Rome. Others were predicting the choice of different candidates, but it was Monseigneur Léger who was chosen by Pope Pius XII. He was consecrated and came to take possession of his See and a new era opened in Montreal.

Archbishop Léger took Montreal by storm. He brought his immense qualities to the service of an increasingly complex Archdiocese. He arrived in the beginning of the fifties when much was happening in and around Montreal. The mentality of the French-Canadians was changing. The years of the "Révolution Tranquille" were the years of rapid development and great sociological change in Quebec society. The Dominican Father Georges-Henri Lévesque's courses at Laval University were producing French-Canadian leaders in the social field. French high schools were being opened, bridging the gap between the elementary schools and the universities for the young French-Canadians.

Léger arrived with his eloquence and his experience. He gave magnificent talks. He appeared to be tireless, going almost everywhere he was invited and giving public lectures and sermons. He set about finding means to help the unemployed and the poor. He engaged a full-time fundraiser at the very beginning so that he could have homes built for the poor, while at the same time providing work for some of the unemployed labourers in the city. He initiated his daily radio broadcast of the Rosary, with his meditations on the various Mysteries. His program was followed by thousands of people in thousands of homes. He was a very colourful man,

Memoirs

and he brought a great deal to the Church in Montreal.

In the beginning the Archbishop tended to be rather conservative with a somewhat heavy ecclesiastical style. It was not long, however, before you could see the change in him. With his intelligent mind Léger easily grasped the multiple sociological and economical problems which were beginning to surface. As a matter of fact, after a few years, Duplessis was reported to have said that he considered himself worse off than when he had had to contend with Charbonneau.

Archbishop Léger analyzed very quickly the exciting possibilites which were opening up in the society of Montreal. He saw the importance of a good Chaplain in the University. He brought a deep and significant philosophy into the work of the Church - a Church which would have to adapt itself to a changing society. Léger had bought himself a house in Lachine where he could meet with some of the leaders of Quebec society, particularly those in Montreal. These men agreed to meet only if they could do so on a level of dialogue and not just listen to Léger talk. It was under those circumstances that they held sessions occasionally, discussing the role of the Church and the role of politics and business in a society which was becoming radically different.

As the Archbishop, Léger brought a wonderful gift to Montreal and did much that was constructive. It was no surprise to any of us really when, a few years later, he was named a Cardinal. This was a departure from past history because previously the Cardinal had always been in Quebec City. In those days there were two Cardinals in Canada, one English-speaking and one French-speaking. When the Archbishop of Montreal became a Cardinal, there was some jealousy among the old guard in Quebec. They felt that they had been superceded. That was rectified later, however, when once again Quebec was given a Cardinal in the person of Cardinal Maurice Roy.

I had known Léger vaguely at first and then a little better as the years went on. My first contact with him was while I was attending the Collège de Montréal. Léger had returned from Japan after having spent a year there as a missionary. The students from the College were brought in and seated on chairs in the main aisle of the Seminary Chapel. Father Léger said the Mass and gave a sermon. I still remember how impressed I was - so impressed in fact, that I almost thought of becoming a missionary myself! With his usual eloquence Léger gave us a picture of Japan and the work that was there waiting to be done, work which had been begun centuries before by St. Francis Xavier.

I did not see him again until I was in my first year in the Seminary. One day Father Yelle called me in and told me that Father Léger was arriving with two Japanese students. He was aware that the one named Fukahori was a little older and knew some English. The other student did not know either English or French. Yelle wanted someone who could speak to Fukahori in English so he sent

Memoirs

me, along with a French-Canadian seminarian, to meet Father Léger and the two Japanese students. Later on I was able to help these young men with their studies, especially Latin, with which they had much difficulty.

Though Léger was no stranger to me when he came to Montreal, I did have some concern because of the change of the Archbishop. I still felt very badly about that, of course, and I wanted to put all the cards on the table. So at our first meeting, I said, "I am working in the Chancery Office as well as at St. Mary's Hospital. I think I should be very honest and open with you. I admired and loved Archbishop Charbonneau. I was very closely associated with him and with many of the things he did in the Diocese, and I supported him. If there is any judgment against him and his policies, then I must share in that judgment. Perhaps you might prefer to give me some other assignment. I would be willing to accept any change you wish to make. "

Léger was listening intently. He stood up, came over to me and said, "It would be my hope that you would give me the same loyalty and the same affection that you gave to Archbishop Charbonneau."

I said, "Your Grace, you have my loyalty, there is no question about that, and I am certain that as we work together affection will follow."

He smiled. With that decision, I continued working as I had been - at the Chancery Office and St. Mary's Hospital.

Alex Carter

My relationship with the Cardinal in those days was very cordial. A few years later, he asked me if I would accept to be Pastor of Holy Family Parish because he was very concerned about it. The parish had been in difficulty for many years. Archbishop Léger had received a delegation of people from the parish and they were practically in despair. So when he asked me if I would consider the appointment, I said, "Certainly. I would be glad to go if that is what you want." By this time I also thought I might enjoy a new challenge.

Thus began the next phase of my life. I was to leave the hospital and the Chancery. I continued to do some work for the Tribunal, but that was just two or three afternoons a week. My main concern for the next two and a half years would be Holy Family Parish.

Holy Family had existed for some twenty-nine or more years, serving the English-speaking Catholic people over a vast area in northeast Montreal. I spent a delightful couple of years there, and with my two assistants, Father Walter Sutton and Father Dick King, we were able to change things in the parish and to restore the confidence of the parishioners. I am glad to say that, even before Vatican II, I challenged the lay people to take more responsibility. I started a parish council. In those days a parish council was not elected but appointed. Under the Quebec system, we had the *Marguillers* -"wardens" of the parish, we would say in English - who legally had to take responsibility

Memoirs

with the parish priest for the financial affairs of the parish. (*Marguillers* was the legal word used in French law.) We built up a very good parish council comprised of both men and women, with representation from every organization in the parish.

Taking a leaf out of Father McShane's book, I visited all of the seventh and eighth grades and talked to the boys individually about vocations and asked them if they had given any consideration to entering the priesthood. I formed a club for those who were interested. Later on, after my departure, a few of them entered the Seminary. I was glad to learn that some of them were eventually ordained and they were doing very good work in the Montreal area.

At that time there was not the shortage of priests that we have today. As I said, I had two assistants at Holy Family. Walter Sutton happened to be an old friend from the Seminary. I consider him as having been one of my greatest friends. We had met regularly when I was at St. Mary's, where he used to come and have dinner with me about once a week. We relaxed together, took trips, discussed our problems and had a lot of fun. It was a friendship that was very enriching. I look back on it with much affection.

Father Sutton succeeded me at Holy Family at my request. I think the Cardinal had other plans, but I pleaded that Wally be my successor. I remember saying to the Cardinal, "Your Eminence, I was the head of Holy Family but Father Sutton was the heart. I may have directed the parish, but he was the one who was beloved by the parishioners in a special way, and I know why. It is because his heart is as big as himself."

I am glad to say that after I left, Wally was able to continue to build up the parish. Holy Family had been a basement church for years. The parishioners collected enough money to get permission to build the church for which they had been saving, a church that had long been desired by the people.

***

It was while I was at Holy Family, in late November of 1956, that I received a call from Cardinal Léger telling me that the Apostolic Delegate, Archbishop Giovanni Panico, was in town and wanted to meet with me that evening.

When Panico arrived, he sat down and began talking to me in both English and French, switching back and forth. After a pleasant conversation he told me the reason for our meeting. He had received a request from Rome that he make an enquiry concerning what had happened to the national paper, *The Ensign*. I gave him the story as I recalled it. He took some notes and thanked me very much. After he left I never thought of it again.

To my immense surprise I received a call from Ottawa shortly after that and was told that I was to report to the Apostolic Delegation. Archbishop Panico said that there were some points he wanted to clear up about the *Ensign* and told me he wanted me to come to Ottawa for lunch. I agreed, knowing there was a train departing mid-morning. I thought I would have time to celebrate the scheduled first Friday Mass to which the children of the school were invited. That day I think every child was at Mass! We always had a large number of school children in attendance, but on that day there seemed to be more than ever. It took me much longer to get out of the church than I had anticipated, so I missed the train. I telephoned the Delegate to say I would be late, but he assured me that it did not make any difference. I got into my car and drove to Ottawa.

When I arrived, I joined the Delegate and his staff for lunch, and then Panico brought me into his office and told me the real reason why he had called me. Tricky little fellow! He informed me that the Holy Father had decided to name me the Coadjutor Bishop of Sault Ste. Marie Diocese, with right of succession. The appointment was dated December 10, 1956. He said that Bishop Dignan was very ill and had been ill for some time and there was an immediate need for a new Bishop.

My response was, "I do not even know where the Sault Diocese is! I know nothing about that part of the country or that part of Ontario. I am sure they must have priests there who are better qualified and more capable."

Panico became a little annoyed and said, "So, are you not willing to do what the Holy Father wants you to do? Are you not willing to serve the Church in the way the Pope thinks you should?"

"Sure, I am willing - if that is the decision, but I just wonder what I can bring to them."

"You have a vast experience in the Church already. I am familiar with your curriculum vitae."

"Fine," I said. "If that is the decision of the Holy Father then I accept."

As anyone might well imagine, to say that this was a surprise would be an understatement. The whole thing was a real shock to me! After my experience in Winnipeg, and then living through the Charbonneau affair in Montreal, I had no desire to be a Bishop. But the decision was made without me and I think, in those times, that was pretty well the order of the day. We had been well trained by the Sulpicians never to question such a decision. I began to prepare myself, therefore, to leave behind my clerical life in the city of Montreal and to accept the new responsibilities being entrusted to me.

Called to be Bishop

Apparently there had been much speculation about the succession to Bishop Ralph Hubert Dignan. Because he was very ill, the poor man was in the hospital more than he was at the Pro-Cathedral Rectory. He was suffering from a very serious heart condition and frequently went into congestive heart failure. It was quite obvious, therefore, and certainly expected, that someone would have to be named soon to attend to the duties which Bishop Dignan would not be able to perform very much longer.

Given the nature of the Diocese of Sault Ste. Marie, with almost equivalent numbers of English-speaking and French-speaking Catholics, the desire among the Francophones for a French-Canadian Bishop had always been an issue, and this time there were serious efforts made to have one named. Cardinal Léger told me later that even he had received a delegation from the Sault Ste. Marie Diocese. A few professional people and some educators had come to see him privately, asking him to use his influence to ensure that the one who would succeed Bishop Dignan would be a French-Canadian.

I have to say that when I arrived in North Bay I did not really feel welcomed by Bishop Dignan. He was very polite when I met him, but he was not very warm. He had already chosen the man he would have liked to succeed him and had indicated his preference so, when I was named, I am sure he must have been very disappointed. I first travelled to North Bay to meet him around the New Year, and he was waiting up when my train arrived about nine o'clock at night. I had intended to stay three or four days, but after an hour or so of conversation, I realized there was not much point in my staying. I told Father Francis Devine, the Rector, that I had changed my plans; I was going back to Montreal the next day on the train. Mind you, all was not lost. That brief visit gave me a chance to meet the priests at the Pro-Cathedral: Frank Devine, Bernard Pappin, Richard Allen and James Cashubec. I was warmly welcomed by them and I liked the atmosphere around the rectory.

I returned to Montreal and Archbishop Léger consecrated me on February 2, 1957 in Notre Dame Basilica - that beautiful building which represents so much of the history of Montreal. Bishop Dignan was there and he and Bishop Whelan, the Auxiliary of Montreal, were Co-Consecrators, as they were called in those days. It was a beautiful ceremony.

Memoirs

I then made my final preparations for leaving Montreal to take up my duties as Coadjutor Bishop of the Diocese of Sault Ste. Marie. As an example of the kind of Church-State relations that existed at that time in Montreal, the Canadian National Railway was gracious enough to place a railway car at my disposal. There were about four or five compartments on it for myself and my family. Many of my Montreal friends wanted to accompany me to my reception in North Bay, so the delegation which came with me filled two cars. The parlour car was taken off the train in North Bay and put on a side rail where it remained until twelve o'clock that night. After the reception, the Trans-Canada was to pick it up and take the family back to Montreal, where they would arrive at nine o'clock the next morning. I would remain in North Bay, of course, and that was to be the final break with my long twenty-one years of service to the Church as a priest in Montreal.

My formal reception at the Pro-Cathedral of the Assumption in North Bay, where the Bishop of the Diocese of Sault Ste. Marie had always lived, was very nicely organized by Father Devine, the Rector. I was met at the door of the Pro-Cathedral by the Bishop, by Monsignor T. J. Crowley, who was much revered by the English-speaking community, and by Monseigneur Oscar Racette, the distinguished representative of the French-speaking community. They brought me up the aisle. Bishop Dignan went to his throne and I was ushered to my place in the sanctuary. The Bishop officiated at the Mass and welcomed me in the sermon. It was a nice welcome, up to the point where, for the first time, he referred to me as Bishop Cartier. I did not know whether it was by error or design. A little later, when he referred to me again as Bishop Cartier, I was pretty well persuaded that it was by design.

As a matter of fact, my brother Emmett had the same impression because he said to me right after the ceremony, "I think you are going to have a bit of difficulty. I don't think that was done by accident."

I said, "I'm afraid I have to agree. I don't know whether he was just trying to be funny or whether he was trying to drive a wedge between myself and the English-speaking community in the Diocese. It will be interesting to watch and see what happens."

As the months went by, I did not see much of Bishop Dignan. I was on the road most of the time and Bishop Dignan spent a great deal of time in the hospital. When we were together at the rectory, our exchanges were always very polite. Whenever the Bishop came home, Father Cashubec, who was on staff at the Pro-Cathedral, was very generous with his services and brought him around in a wheel-chair.

Shortly after I arrived in the Diocese, the Bishop antagonized the Apostolic Delegate unnecessarily. He had invited Archbishop Panico sometime earlier to come and tour the Diocese. Bishop Dignan had been in the hospital and when Panico arrived he came out of the hospital to welcome him officially at the Church. I think he was ill-advised to do so. He was wheeled down the centre aisle of the Pro-Cathedral, welcomed the Delegate there and then was wheeled back up the aisle. Afterwards he asked for a meeting with the Delegate. I was in the recreation room where we were having a little libation before dinner. After their meeting, Archbishop Panico and Bishop Dignan joined us for a few minutes. I could see that the Apostolic Delegate was very upset. After dinner we went back to the recreation room to relax. Bishop Dignan had gone to bed, and Panico said he wanted to talk to me alone. He was furious.

He said, "I asked Bishop Dignan about the situation in Elliot Lake. There are approximately ten thousand French-Canadian people there who have been asking for a parish for two or three years. He will not give them any answer and he will not receive them. Do you know what he said to me?" he fumed. "He said that these people have to learn to wait a few years. In his opinion you never give in to them right away. You just make them wait. You take your time."

Since I had not been involved in this issue at all and knew nothing about it, I said I found this a rather surprising attitude, but I could not make any judgment because I did not know the background or any of the details. I had just arrived in the Diocese and had been very busy with Confirmations.

Alex Carter

Because of the Bishop's illness, he had missed Confirmations for several years. There was a long list of children waiting for this Sacrament, particularly in the French-speaking parishes. In fact, in Sudbury, there were over four hundred children from St. Jean de Brébeuf Parish alone. The new church was just on the point of being built and the basement would never have accommodated that many. We had to move to the Collège du Sacré Coeur (Sacred Heart College), not far from the church, and use the gymnasium. I swore to myself that I would never do that again. In those days, the entire ceremony was in Latin, including the formula. By the time I had Confirmed over half of the children, I was almost dizzy. With so many children to annoint and bless while saying the formula, it was a struggle not to confuse the wording.

Again, the Bishop's illness made it impossible for him to accompany the Delegate as far as Sault Ste. Marie. I had to take his place and go across the Diocese with Panico. I think the Delegate was impressed with what he saw. Certainly the faith of our people was very evident. The turn-out to greet him was good. It was, I think, a successful tour. Nonetheless, Panico was still fuming about the Elliot Lake situation and I knew that the Bishop had done himself a lot of harm.

I must say I felt very sorry for Bishop Dignan. Not only was he in very bad health, but he was unable to adapt to the new vision of Church which I detected growing among the priests of the Diocese.

Memoirs

Many of the older Bishops found themselves with similar pastoral problems.

In a lighter vein, around that time, a problem arose concerning one of our seminarians who was studying at St. Augustine's Seminary in Toronto. Towards the end of his studies, Brian McKee and the Rector were not seeing eye to eye. Brian, who had earlier taken a year off, was thinking of discontinuing his studies for the priesthood. I was asked by Bishop Dignan to deal with this because, if Brian was to be ordained, he would be responsible to me before long. I saw the promise in the man, and due to the fact that he did not have the full approval of St. Augustine's, I decided to establish our own Seminary - St. Mary's of the Lake - in North Bay. Because most of his academic studies had been completed at St. Augustine's, with the help of some of the priests of the Cathedral and Chancery staff, I saw to his final preparations for ordination. Bishop Dignan ordained him to the priesthood in April of that year. Immediately afterwards we closed the Seminary, so it has the unique distinction, I suppose, of having only one alumnus. We have been one hundred percent successful, so far!

I had come to the Diocese in March, on the feast of St. Thomas, which was then celebrated on the seventh of March, and in October I was invited to speak at the National Social Life Conference. In those days, we had our annual Conference in different places across the country. This time it was in St. John, New Brunswick and I had been asked to give a talk there, on the second day, to the professional men of St. John.

Upon my arrival I received a call from Archbishop Panico saying, "Alex, you must come to Ottawa immediately."

"What do you mean 'immediately'?" I asked.

"I mean right now. As soon as you can get away."

"Well, just a minute," I said, "I have to give a talk tomorrow to the lawyers, doctors and professional men of St. John. Is it alright if I tell them I have received an urgent call from the Apostolic Delegate?"

"Oh, no, no, you cannot mention that."

"And, I can't walk out on a conference either."

"So, when can you come?" he asked.

"My talk is tomorrow morning. I will be finished by noon and I will leave as soon as possible after that. I should arrive in Ottawa either tomorrow afternoon or the next day at the latest."

In Ottawa, Panico told me that Rome had named me the Administrator of the Diocese of Sault Ste. Marie. Personally, I think that if, during Panico's trip to the Sault, Bishop Dignan had been

Memoirs

well enough to receive the Delegate himself and travel through the Diocese with him, things might have turned out differently. As it was, I had to return from Ottawa with papers advising Bishop Dignan that I was now the Administrator of the Diocese and that Archbishop Panico had ordered me to take over immediately.

I think Bishop Dignan was justifiably hurt by these abrupt and unexpected developments. It was a very unpleasant task for me to have to perform. Bishop Dignan was in the hospital and I had to go and present him with the document from Rome. Having read it, he said "So that's the way it is."

I told him I was sorry; that this was not at my request and that I had nothing to do with it.

"It doesn't matter," he answered. "I am going to leave anyway. I am going home to London."

"You don't have to do that. Keep your rooms in the rectory. There is no reason for you to leave at all," I assured him. "I will stay in the room I have down the hall. I do not want you to leave. You have been Bishop here for such a long time. You cannot just pack up and go away."

"No, Bishop Carter. I am going back to London, and you will do the same thing when you retire. You will go back to Montreal."

I told him I didn't think so, but he insisted that I would.

"Well, if there is anything I can do, let me know," I said. I also assured him that the Diocese would take care of his financial needs.

Bishop Dignan went to live with his brother in London and died less than a year later. At the time of his death, Bishop John Cody, the Bishop of London, telephoned me and said that he was rather embarrassed because Bishop Dignan had indicated in his Will that he wanted to be buried in the crypt of St. Peter's Seminary and have his Funeral Mass celebrated in London rather than North Bay.

He asked, "Would you come and say the Mass at least?"

"Of course I will," I said, "and thank you very much. I appreciate your invitation because I think it would be upsetting for our priests and people not to be involved in the funeral of Bishop Dignan. I am also going to encourage our priests to go to London for the Service. It is a pity, you know. There is a place here for the Bishops to be buried in our Cathedral cemetery but he obviously had made up his own mind, and there is nothing I can do about it. However, I will be very happy to go and celebrate the Mass."

***

Memoirs

With Bishop Dignan's death, I automatically became the Bishop of the Diocese of Sault Ste. Marie. I had already made a fairly extensive tour of the Diocese during my role as Coadjutor and I was glad of that. I had taken that opportunity to listen to all the comments and even the complaints of the priests who did not feel obligated to mince their words because they knew I had no authority in the Diocese. The trip had proven to be an excellent source of information. It had also been a means of evaluation from my own point of view. I realized that there were some very big tasks ahead.

Covering the large territory of the Sault Diocese, for any Bishop, is a challenge in that it involves a great deal of travel. During my first year, I think I slept in my own bed about one-sixth of the time. The travelling was instructive and helped me to have at least a bird's eye view of some of the difficulties I would have to face. The two issues that concerned me most were the division between the English-speaking and French-speaking Catholics and the uncertain financial situation of the Diocese.

The French-speaking and English-speaking groups in our Church had not really gelled at all. There was bad feeling between many of them. The Franco-Ontarians felt that they had been discriminated against and I have to say, in all honesty, that I agreed with them. One French-speaking pastor in North Bay said to me after about a year, "I am glad you are here because we felt we had no future if the situation did not change." It was obvious to me that

I would have to ensure that the Francophones played their full role as equal partners in our Church. In my early letters to the priests and faithful, I tried to bring this matter to their attention.

For the most part, it was not usually the people themselves who were quarreling. The greatest antagonism seemed to exist among the leaders of society and the education groups. The right was not always on one side either. There were unfair tactics and prejudices, sometimes on the side of the Francophone group and at other times on the side of the Anglophone group.

I felt we were giving poor Christian witness by being divided and by quarreling among ourselves. It was important to me to try to bring about an attitude of love and respect, and I knew that could not be done overnight. Conversion does not come easily or immediately. There were wide differences of opinion and, in some cases, outright antagonism. On the whole, I would have to say that, although initially there was considerable resistance from some, eventually there was a growing peace and harmony among our priests and people in both sectors.

One of the major projects I undertook in my early years, and one which brought both criticism and acclaim, was the hiring of the Wells Company to run a fund-raising campaign in the Diocese. It was a relatively new form of campaign. The arrangement was that the parishes would keep a

Memoirs

certain amount of the money raised; the poorer parishes the entire amount and the well-to-do parishes only twenty percent or so. The remainder was to be given to the Diocesan Fund, which would be built up and used to help the poor and to meet the educational, spiritual and charitable needs of our Diocese. The campaign was a great success. Apart from the sums of money raised for each of the parishes, the Diocesan Fund ended up with about two and a half million dollars.

As is to be expected where money matters and fund-raising are concerned, there were some people who were not too happy with this idea in the beginning. In the end, however, when our goal was achieved, I think our people were very satisfied and delighted with the results. The Campaign launched our Diocese into taking more seriously our spiritual and moral responsibility to find ways to help the poor and those in need. Financially, the Diocese had turned a corner, so to speak. Until this point we had to scramble and beg to find funds for each critical situation that arose. We now had sufficient financial resources to fall back on and we could face the future with a little more certainty.

I also found, when I first arrived in North Bay as the Bishop of Sault Ste. Marie, that there seemed to be very little communication between Catholics and Protestants. I wanted to remedy that situation, so I decided to adopt the practice of hosting a New Year's "Levee" (Reception) to which we would invite some of the prominent people in the city, including professional people, civic leaders and leaders of various organizations. The Levee became a "feature" for several years. The first year, there was a certain amount of hesitation on the part of some of the people who came, because they had absolutely no idea of what to expect.

The guests were brought up to our reception room and were presented to me. We shook hands and I had a chat with them. Then they would be invited to go downstairs to our dining room to have refreshments. Some were very nervous. They had never met a Bishop before. I remember a rather well-to-do man who was involved in the mining industry. He was powerfully built. When he came in, I shook hands with him and he said, "Bishop Carter, you do not know what it took for me to come in here to see you today. I have never shaken hands with a priest, let alone a Bishop. Did you notice how wet my hand was? I was terrified of coming here but now I am glad I did."

We chatted for a few minutes longer and laughed about a few things. He left saying that this had been a great experience. My only hope was that this small attempt at bringing together both the Protestants and Catholics in the city would lead to a closer relationship between these two groups.

***

Apart from getting to know the priests, the parishes and the people, and performing the regular duties of a bishop in my first years, there were two challenges that had to be faced. The first concerned the University of Sudbury. It had been brought to my attention even before I had been consecrated. I think it was on the very day the news was published that I had been named Coadjutor of Sault Ste. Marie that I received a phone call from Father Alphonse Raymond, S.J., in Sudbury. By using a special Charter that had been given to the Jesuits authorizing them to found Colleges, Father Raymond had been able to override any objection from the Provincial government to having a university in Sudbury. He said that they had decided to start their own university, particularly for the graduates of Sudbury's Collège du Sacré Coeur. I congratulated him on his initiative. He stayed in close touch with me while the university was being organized. It was in a very modest location, in rooms over the Empire Theatre. Nevertheless, it was a break-through and the beginning of a developing university.

Soon, however, the Ontario government became interested in forming a major university in Northern Ontario. There was competition between North Bay and Sudbury to secure that university. After much deliberation Sudbury was chosen because it was larger and it was closer to other centres the government wanted to serve. What was conceived was a university which would recognize the place of the churches. The University of Sudbury, which Father Raymond had begun, would become a Catholic University within the central university for Northern Ontario, later called Laurentian University. Laurentian would also include a University for the United Church and a University for the Anglican Church. The plan also called for affiliated colleges in North Bay, Sault Ste. Marie and Timmins.

Needless to say there were many meetings and discussions about this. I was in Rome in 1959 for my *ad limina* visit and while there I seized the opportunity to go to the Congregation for Universities. I took the precaution of bringing with me Bishop Louis Lévesque, the Bishop of Hearst, who was also in Rome at the time. I also brought one of my priests who was studying in Rome, Father Adolphe Proulx. I told him I wanted him to take notes and to write up the minutes of the meeting. We saw Monsignor Pallatini first and later Monsignor Staffa joined us. I explained the details of the project that we were debating in Sudbury, citing St. Michael's College in Toronto as an example. We were in discussion for quite awhile. Staffa's main concern was that the Catholic character of the University of Sudbury be protected. I assured him that it would be protected by a Board of Directors and that the French Jesuits would be in charge of education as well as the University's policies. Hearing this, Staffa was very expansive in his summation and concluded by stating that he could see no objection. I then asked Adolphe to come with Bishop Lévesque and myself and had him write up the minutes of the meeting, which Bishop Lévesque and I both signed.

Memoirs

Fortunately I had kept those minutes in my file, because not long afterwards, some of the French-speaking educators in Ottawa objected to the plan, in fact, to the whole set-up. They wrote to Archbishop Sebastiano Baggio, the Apostolic Delegate in Ottawa, to try to stop the development of the University of Sudbury.

I met with them several times. Bishop Maxime Tessier of Timmins and Bishop Lévesque were with me at some of those meetings. Their concern was that the presence of the other two universities - Thorneloe, for the Anglicans, and Huntington, for the United Church - would be endangering the faith of the French-Canadian young people. I remember one gentleman in particular who was quite well known in Ottawa and a fine man, but very nationalistic. He and several others felt that it would be sinful to have our young people under the same roof as the "Prédicants Protestants" (the Protestant preachers). We tried to convince them that there was no danger involved. I pointed out that these professors would not be teaching our students unless they happened to be enrolled in some particular courses, but they still objected to what we were proposing.

I received a letter from Archbishop Baggio asking me on what authority we were proceeding with this three-Church type of University which, under the auspices of the government of Ontario and under a University Charter, would be known as Laurentian University. I promptly sent him a copy of the minutes of my meeting in Rome which stated that there was no objection to this; that it had been explained to the Congregation and had been accepted. I told him I thought that the decision to proceed, in view of the fact that there was nothing in principle against it, was now a decision to be made by the Bishop of the Diocese.

Archbishop Baggio, who was always a very good friend of mine, answered. He said he was under the impression, from what he could find out after his inquiries in Rome, that the Congregation had understood it to be more a theoretical question than a practical one.

"That does not change the fact that, in principle, they agreed with what we were doing," I said. I also told him that I knew where the opposition was coming from. Some of the dissenters were affiliated with the University of Ottawa and they wanted to control all of the French-Canadian Catholic higher education in Ontario.

I must say that Premier Leslie Frost was a great supporter of the Laurentian project. He accepted our request that the whole University be bilingual and bicultural, which meant giving classes to students in their own language. Also, the administration of L'Université Laurentienne, Laurentian University, would be set up as an entity which, by its very nature, would be bicultural and bilingual. I wrote down four or five sentences on the nature of the University that I asked to have incorporated into the

Memoirs

Act of the Provincial Legislature when the University Bill appeared and Frost accepted them word for word.

The opening of the University of Sudbury was very timely for Father Raymond's institution. They were able to sell their library and much of their equipment to the new Laurentienne and pay off their considerable debt. In so doing, they obviously sacrificed a certain amount of independence but they gained a much greater importance by becoming part of this broader university which was going to serve a large part of Northern Ontario. In fact, the Rector of this new University of Sudbury, Father Emile Bouvier, S.J., was actually named the President of Laurentian University, a position he held for its first year.

Father Lucien Matte, S.J., became President of the University of Sudbury in 1962. He wanted to raise money, especially for a student's residence. I accompanied him to see a few warm-hearted and prominent Catholic people who responded generously. We also had a successful fund-raising campaign in our parishes in Northern Ontario and the Jesuits contributed whatever salaries they received. Not only did this combined effort enable us to achieve our goal, but I am convinced that it was a unifying force in the community. The University of Sudbury Board of Regents brought together both English-speaking and French-speaking Catholics who were friendly and cooperative, working together for this one institution which served both the Francophone and the Anglophone population.

This joint effort showed that, when there is mutual respect, people can work together and there can be harmony and unity of purpose. This friendship and mutual cooperation has continued to exist between the Jesuits, most of whom are from Quebec, and the Francophone and Anglophone men and women who have served on the Board of Regents of the University of Sudbury.

***

The second major challenge that I had to deal with in addition to my own normal duties was the 1958 Inco strike called by the workers of the Mine-Mill Union. Unfortunately the Mine-Mill had sent some six million dollars to the United States to fight against the Smith Bill that was being opposed by left-wingers. As a result they had very little money to back their own strike and to help provide for their striking workers. Inco was very strong at that time. They had the resources and they had the money. They were determined to sit out the strike, even though it would be costly for them because nickel was in demand and the price was high. The strike was a long one and it caused a great deal of hardship in Sudbury.

I called for a collection in the churches of the Diocese. I had some very active priests in Sudbury. I think of Father J.J. Delaney of St. Bartholomew's Church in Levack, and the parish priest of Christ the King, Monsignor J.C. Humphrey and so many others who volunteered to help. We set up food banks and collected clothing for families. We gave all the help we could. In the meantime, the strike dragged on and on. There were meetings in Toronto. Premier Frost was in touch with me several times. I had his private number; he had mine. In our discussions I encouraged him to use his influence with Inco to bring an end to this very unfortunate situation that was affecting so many of our families, especially the women and children. After having been accustomed to a fairly good salary, these workers and their families suddenly found themselves living on a pittance. The strike was a long and wearing experience for all. Eventually, the women called a meeting at the Sudbury arena to protest that the Union was not doing enough to try to bring the strike to an end.

I have not forgotten the very kind gestures of Bishop Gérard-Marie Coderre of St. Jean, who sent me a cheque for ten thousand dollars to help the families affected by the strike, and Bishop John C. Cody of London, who also sent me a cheque through the diocesan St. Vincent de Paul Society. The next time I went to the Canadian Bishops' meeting, the strike had just ended. I was so surprised at the meeting when many of the Quebec Bishops came up to shake hands with me, telling me how much they admired my courage and the things I was doing in Sudbury. Then it dawned on me what had inspired their warm congratulations and remarks about courage. They were still thinking about Archbishop Charbonneau, who had taken up collections for the strikers during the Asbestos strike, and they knew I had gone ahead and done likewise. Some of them probably thought I might be joining Charbonneau in Victoria, but anyway they were very effusive in their praise!

I was also heartened and encouraged at that time by the articles of Fathers Gérard Dion and Louis O'Neil in their *Cahiers,* their Social Action publications. These men were leaders in the field of unionized labour and they were concerned with strengthening the workers, protecting them, and working for laws to that effect. They were graduates of Father Georges-Henri Lévesque's Faculty of Social Science at Laval University, and their support was most encouraging.

It was in that spirit that I sent a letter to pastors saying that, for building churches and for major repairs, I wanted them to use unionized labour. I also asked that, in places where unionized labour was not available, for example in the small villages around Nipissing or Algoma, that they would still observe the standard union wages for anyone they were hiring. This action brought rather negative reactions from some of the priests of the Diocese. A little education had to be done along that line in those days. It also brought a letter from Father George Higgins - later Monsignor Higgins - who was the head of the Department for Social Justice for the American Bishops. He informed me that from Washington he had sent out copies of my letter in several languages. That was my first contact with Monsignor Higgins. Through that little incident we became good friends and we would meet again later on in Rome, during the Council.

When the strike was finally settled, the aftermath became somewhat controversial. The Steel Workers Union was making a bid to take over at Inco. As I mentioned earlier, the Mine-Mill had weakened their position, having called the strike after spending so much money on a purely American and ideological cause, the Smith Bill. Meanwhile the University of Sudbury decided that there should be a course provided to educate our workers. They brought in Professor Alexandre Boudreau from the Maritimes to give the course. He trained them in the true principles of unionism and encouraged them to become leaders in their unions. The course was also designed to provide the workers with some practical strategies. They were given some expertise in expressing themselves so that they need not allow only a few people to dominate their union. They were made aware of the use of unfair procedural tactics and how to deal with them. Later, the University of Sudbury and I were accused of trying to break up the Mine-Mill Union because some of the people who had taken the course had worked to bring the Steel Workers Union to Sudbury. This accusation was not true; nor was this the purpose of the course. We were simply trying to help the workers to take their responsibilities within the union movement.

***

Alex Carter

The appeal of Pope John XXIII to the Church on the North American continent, especially in the United States and Canada, to send some priests to Latin America was taken very seriously by our Canadian Conference. The Canadian Bishops had earlier participated in the establishment of a school for language and missionary studies in Mexico and the religious communities of Canada had cooperated fully. Also, under the auspices of the Canadian Conference, the Bishops had helped in Latin America by establishing a Seminary in Honduras where the local students could be trained.

As for our own Diocese, I think that one of the best things we did during the years of my active ministry was to answer this appeal in 1961. We took an interest in the Church in Latin America by adopting a mission to be staffed by our priests. Because the need was so great, the Pope told us it would bring a blessing upon our own dioceses if we helped the dioceses of Latin America. That was what we in the Sault Ste. Marie Diocese undertook to do. Although we were not blessed with an overabundance of priests to meet our own diocesan needs, we were certainly in better shape than they were in Latin America. It was a matter of duty for me to try to respond to the Holy Father's request. Our priests cooperated beautifully and several of them volunteered to learn the language and to serve in Latin America. Our people supported them fully, and our local parishes were very generous in providing financial assistance.

Memoirs

We were not alone in our generosity. Most other Canadian dioceses were working out agreements with local Bishops in Latin America, or working with some particular group to decide how and where they could best render service. I think our Canadian Bishops were very anxious to help in whatever way they could. They were all very generous in trying to respond to our Holy Father's appeal. John XXIII was such a wonderful man. You had to be touched by his compassion.

Knowing very little about Latin America, I too needed advice about where our Diocese could best serve. I decided to consult with some Bishops from the United States and Latin America and with the Scarboro Foreign Missions Society in Toronto. At home there was some pressure to choose Guatemala because the Sisters of St. Joseph had a boarding school in North Bay and several Guatemalan youngsters had been sent there by their parents. Since we had some working knowledge of that country, Guatemala seemed a logical choice. I then consulted with the American missionaries who were in Guatemala at the time, the Maryknoll Fathers. These men advised me to choose between two Bishops whose dioceses were in grave need. One was Bishop Luna of Zacapa; the other was Bishop Manresa from Quezaltenango. I met with the two of them in Guatemala to discuss the decision. Bishop Manresa was very objective and extremely charitable. He told me that his needs were immense but he felt that, in conscience, he had to advise me that Bishop Luna's needs were even greater. That was when I chose to send our priests to the Zacapa Diocese.

I always seemed to have trouble with Nuncios. I ran into trouble with the Nuncio to Guatemala who objected to my choice of Diocese because I made it without going through him. He became very vehement. I had to insist upon my choice and it all ended up in Rome finally. It was rather tense for awhile. Since I had to go to Rome on other business, I went to the Congregation of the Propagation of the Faith while I was there. I spoke to the Cardinal Prefect and told him that if I had any more trouble I would simply not send my men to Guatemala at all. Furthermore, I would make a statement explaining why I was not sending them. Happily, that put an end to any misunderstanding. As a matter of fact, the Prefect was very accommodating, assuring me that he would arrange everything. I was not to worry because he was very happy that I was offering to send some of my priests to help in Bishop Luna's diocese. Eventually even the Nuncio to Guatemala agreed to accept whatever help I was willing to give to the Diocese of my choice.

The first of our priests to serve in Latin America was Father Conway McKee, who did a magnificent job in opening the mission in the parish of Gualan. He was joined by other priests as time went on - James Cashubec, Jean-Marie Paiement, Harris Mulcahey, David Cresswell, Frank Farenzena, Jack David, Frank Folz, Norm Fortier and Donald Tait -

and they expanded the mission to include the parishes of Teculutan and La Union. These men were very fine and I was so proud of them. When I visited Latin America it was a real joy to see what they were accomplishing.

Parish work was the main concern of our priests. Their pastoral ministry was not limited to their own town parishes, but included almost countless numbers of tiny villages. Many of these "aldeas" were accessible only by mule or on horseback. In addition, these priests did an immense amount of social education. The Coffee Co-op which they helped the people to establish in La Union was one major example. It became recognized as a producer of first class coffee. That was really an achievement. They also set up a Credit Union for the people of the area.

I have always been extremely grateful for the dedication and generous service of the women religious of our Diocese. That same generosity was evident when the Sisters of St. Joseph of Sault Ste. Marie, with the encouragement of their Mother General, Sister St. Edward, and her Council, agreed to join us in Guatemala. The Sisters arrived shortly after we opened the mission and founded a school in Gualan. The school was not only for children but it was a base for adult education as well. The Sisters also became involved in health care and set up a clinic in the town. They too established a Credit Union for the people of Gualan and the surrounding area. Usually three or four Sisters were assigned at a time to their Mission in Gualan and over the years a total of sixteen Sisters of St. Joseph served there until they closed the Mission in 1978.

I have to mention particularly the very great help that our men received from Irving and Gladys Stahl who lived in Guatemala City. That Catholic couple were so kind and generous. Our priests were susceptible to infections while they were in Guatemala. Whenever they became ill and needed time off, the Stahls would receive them into their home and care for them. They were certainly the best friends, I think, that our priests ever made in Guatemala. I myself thoroughly enjoyed spending time with them whenever I went down to visit our mission.

One time the Canadian Ambassador in Guatemala City gave a dinner in my honour to acknowledge the great contribution that had been made by the Diocese of Sault Ste. Marie in Guatemala. It was a lovely banquet. He had invited a number of special guests from around the city. As I was chatting with the Ambassador, sitting next to him on his right, he said, "You know, Bishop Carter, I wrote to our government and said that if a decision had to be made to close either our Embassy or the missions of the Diocese of Sault Ste. Marie, we should close the Embassy." That Ambassador was the distinguished Canadian diplomat, Saul Rae, whose son Bob became the Premier of Ontario in 1990.

Memoirs

A few years after we had established our mission, Bishop Joseph Ryan of Hamilton wanted to send a priest to serve in Guatemala. He only had one, so he asked me if this man could work with our group. I said "Of course" and that priest took over the parish of Teculutan. Shortly after, when I suggested to Bishop Ryan that the Hamilton Diocese reimburse us for what our Diocese had spent in establishing the parish, he declined. When I persisted, he laughed and said, in his own inimitable way, " So, sue me."

We left a splendid record in Latin America. I had told our priests that we were not a missionary society. We were going to need them back home. They were each allotted a period of five years and my plan had been that we should be out of Guatemala in a reasonable length of time. I asked the priests to try to find vocations, and I am glad to say that during our time in Guatemala, they did so. The pastors chose promising candidates, put them through college and sent them to the Seminary. Two of them persevered, and when their preparation was complete, they were ordained to the priesthood. With these newly ordained priests, the Diocese of Zacapa would be able to take over their own parishes of Gualan and La Union. Our goal had been achieved, and we gradually brought our men back home. The last of our missionary priests returned to our Diocese in 1979. We had replaced our own clergy with young ordained Guatemalans, young men who would never have become priests without the influence and the presence of our Sault priests.

I still often talk about the great work accomplished by our priests and the lasting friendships they formed. One of the priests from Zacapa Diocese, Anibal Casasola, one of their former altar boys who eventually became pastor in Gualan, still comes up to visit occasionally. The link with Guatemala still remains, by virtue of the relationships formed and the fact that our Diocese continues to support them somewhat financially.

The development of our Latin American mission, I believe, brought a great blessing to our Diocese. I also believe that the whole Canadian contribution at that time answered in a creditable and generous way the appeal of the Holy Father.

***

I always felt that I received much support from the priests in the Diocese of Sault Ste. Marie. When I first arrived, there were many of them with great experience who familiarized me with the history of the Diocese since its establishment in 1904. They spoke of the times of Bishop David Joseph Scollard and Bishop Dignan and the growth and development of the Diocese. I greatly appreciated that.

I was most unfortunate, however, in the fact that within a few years after my arrival, I lost three of the men who had been most helpful to me. One was Monsignor J.C. Humphrey, a great Churchman. He had at one time been Chancellor and also Rector of the Pro-Cathedral in North Bay. Then there was

Memoirs

Monsignor Frank Devine who was Rector of the Pro-Cathedral when I arrived and who had taken over Christ the King Church in Sudbury after Humphrey's death. Frank was certainly doing a tremendous job of bringing the parish a new form of leadership, and a very effective one. Cut down in the fullness of his early years, he was only forty-three when he died suddenly in his sleep. It was a shocking experience. The third, Monseigneur Lorenzo Coté, who was my right hand man in the French sector, did not die but he became very ill. The task of completing the building of the very large Church of St. Jean de Brébeuf in Sudbury and his concern about the enormous debt on it, seemed to take its toll. So, effectively, I was deprived of his active and loyal support.

***

One of my first steps after I became Bishop was to organize the Chancery Office, with Fathers Adolphe Proulx and Bernard Pappin as Chancellors; the former responsible for spiritual affairs and the latter responsible for temporal affairs. I asked Adolphe to go to the Chancery Office in Montreal and Bernard to go to the Chancery in London to gain some practical experience. The following year I sent Adolphe to Rome to study Canon Law and later sent Bernard to Rome for studies in Theology. With that background they helped me to set up our office. Father Cashubec, who had had no formal training or practical experience at all in Tribunal work, was given the responsibility of establishing an Officiality. I gave him some books to read and we discussed pertinent questions and issues. With my own knowledge of Tribunal work, I was able to give him some guidance and I was amazed at how quickly he learned and how efficient he became.

In those early years, I was also concerned about the health of my priests. They were hard working men. I made a rule that every priest was to take a day off each week. My reason for making it a rule was to ensure that no pastor could object to his assistant or assistants having a free day. That rule was much appreciated, especially by the younger and more vigorous priests. Strangely enough, this would be indirectly responsible for the beginning of the Flying Fathers hockey team, a story which is worth telling.

The weekly day off for Father Brian McKee, who was by then an assistant at the Pro-Cathedral in North Bay, was always spent with his great friend Les Costello, from the Timmins Diocese, who was stationed in Cobalt. McKee and Costello would begin their day by celebrating Mass for the Sisters of the Precious Blood at six-thirty in the morning. After this the two of them would drive to the Ted Reese Arena in Toronto for eleven o'clock to play hockey with the Toronto priests. When the game was over, they would "grab a hot dog" and drive to Blue Mountain near Collingwood to ski until about four-thirty in the afternoon! After supper, the two would end the day by taking in a movie or a game

Memoirs

at the Gardens. Then, of course, they had to drive back to North Bay and they never arrived home until about three in the morning. This was the routine of these energetic young priests every winter Thursday for three years!

On one of those trips to Toronto, Father McKee asked the Toronto priests if they would come to North Bay to play a benefit hockey game for a little boy who had lost an eye in sports. They readily agreed and played a team sponsored by the Continental Hotel. It was a serious game and the priests won 7-4. When the skates came off, however, it was clear that the team had captured more ink and publicity than fans in the seats, although they did raise seven hundred dollars.

In fact, the press, the radio station and especially the TV station played up the event so much that the priests were almost compelled to have a repeat performance, which they did, of course, against a news media team in North Bay.

The media really hammed it up even though some of them could hardly skate. For their part in the promotion, the priests invited some of the older local pastors to play on their team - men who were definitely never regarded as NHL prospects. The evening was a huge success. The arena was full. We all enjoyed some good hockey mixed with hilarious antics. There were pies in the face, phony water buckets and even a "flying nun".

The media christened the priests' team the "Flying Fathers". And so began, in 1964, the hockey team of Roman Catholic priests that would become world famous and go on to entertain all over Canada, Germany, France and the United States as far as Alaska.

I was honoured to be their first coach, but I think they had an ulterior motive in naming me. How could I tell the priests, once they were enjoying increasing fame, that they could not waste time travelling the country playing hockey, when I had encouraged them initially and been their coach at home!

***

Much of my time in those first few years in the Diocese was given to the on-going struggle to develop the University of Sudbury. In 1959 I was invited to become the Chancellor. I accepted because it was very important that the University fulfill the purpose for which it had been founded and incorporated into the Laurentian complex, namely, that it would be a bilingual and bicultural Catholic University within Laurentian. It was stated very clearly at the time, that I was not being chosen because I was Bishop of the Diocese, since the University did not want to create a precedent. They wanted to reserve for themselves the right to name whomever they wished as Chancellor.

Memoirs

I am very happy to note that upon my retirement the University once again decided to name the Bishop of the Diocese as Chancellor, also on the understanding that it was a personal invitation and appointment. It pleased me that my successor as Chancellor would be Bishop Marcel Gervais. His academic background and his work in education were attributes that made their choice a wise one.

***

While I was so intensely involved in building up the life of our local Church, Sault Ste. Marie Diocese, I was forced to make a radical shift in my focus and priorities. Unexpectedly, in 1959, Pope John XXIII called the Second Vatican Council for the universal Church, and the Bishops of the world were asked to prepare for Vatican II. This Council would prove to be full of challenges and surprises. I was about to enter into a process which would profoundly influence my life and my ministry.

The Second Vatican Council

The very suggestion of a Council had come like a stroke of lightning. At that time, no one in their wildest imagination would have thought that a Council would be called. Pius XII had raised the question in the latter years of his Pontificate and had been dissuaded from doing so by those around him. It is certainly no great secret that, in the past, the Cardinal Prefects and Staffs of the Congregations - what we would call the Offices of the Roman Curia - have never been too anxious to have a Council. A Council gives rise to discussions and some disagreements concerning the way the affairs of the Church are being conducted. Needless to say, the Congregations do not feel comfortable when the Bishops of the world convene and offer free advice on how certain situations should be handled, how certain things should be changed or where new directions should be taken. There is nothing unusual about that. The same situation exists in practically every milieu. Certainly the civil service of any country is never too happy when those who are making policies begin to examine the ways and means in which their directives and decisions are being carried out.

When Vatican Council II was called in January 1959, the Canadian Bishops undertook the task of gathering together a team of Canadian theologians who would help the Bishops prepare position papers on the various topics that were to be discussed at the Council. They were also to respond to the preliminary or Pre-Conciliar documents that would be coming to all the Conferences of Bishops around the world. In addition, some of our Bishops asked that their own theologians be allowed to participate in the preparations for the Council. This request was welcomed because we wanted to submit well-prepared proposals that reflected the thinking of all the Canadian Bishops.

***

The Canadian Bishops assembled an excellent team of theological experts. We had chosen Jean-Marie Tillard, O.P., who went on to be famous, one might say, for his contribution to the Ecumenical dialogue, not only with ARCIC (the Anglican-Roman Catholic International Commission), but with other Christian Churches as well. Father Gregory Baum, another notable theologian, was one of those who had been recommended and he came to Ottawa to help in the discussions. We also had a fine team from Montreal, especially those who came with Cardinal Léger's entourage. These men and many others helped a great deal in preparing us for the rather surprising turn that the Council would take. This preparation of the Canadian Bishops was very important. We had new ideas presented to us by our theologians. We were challenged to address the problems that our Church was facing in the world today. These men were familiar with the writings of all the outstanding theologians of our time, some of whom had fallen under suspicion by the Holy Office. I might add that, as time went by in the Council, some of those who had been suspect earlier made a great contribution to the debates and to the decisions that were taken by the Council Fathers.

The Bishops of the world had been invited to send their ideas to Rome concerning which problems and topics should be considered in the Council. Even a cursory look at the immense volumes of submissions from individual Bishops was enough to show the vast differences in concerns and the challenge this would present for the Council.

***

International Commissions were established to help prepare for the Council. My appointment by Rome to the Pre-Conciliar Commission on the Laity was an unexpected and demanding assignment. This meant that periodically I had to go to Rome for meetings in order to study the documents that were being prepared for us. We had an interesting group. Bishop Fulton Sheen, well-known for his American television program, was one of the members of the Commission. So was George Higgins with whom I had only corresponded previously. As I have already mentioned we became good friends. Another was Canon Joseph Cardijn, the founder of the *Jeunesse Ouvrière Chrétienne* and the hero of the workers in Belgium, who brought a wealth of experience to the Commission on the Laity. His interventions were based upon personal experience and personal knowledge.

Unfortunately, I found the process rather disappointing and frustrating. The discussions were strictly theoretical with the exception of the contributions of one or two people who got down to brass tacks. It was very much dominated from the top even though we did have a good chairman, dear old Cardinal Cento, who was quite open-minded. I found very little in the debates and the exchanges that was attuned to the appeals of Pius XI and Pius XII calling for greater participation by the laity in the work of the Church. For instance, I remember the first draft so well - and we had worked on that draft for a long time. It was, for the most part, a timid and flat reiteration of the old principles of Catholic Action, despite the fact that great advances had already been made in many dioceses, including my former Archdiocese of Montreal. The Commission had drawn up a draft of about seventy-five or eighty pages. I read the final text shortly before it was to be presented and I felt obligated to criticize it very strongly. I had taken the trouble to count the number of times in the draft that we had written "cum permissu Episcopi", "with the permission of the Bishop" or "having informed the Bishop" or "with the approval of the Bishop".

In my intervention to the Commission I said, "You know, reading this draft I could come to only one conclusion. We are afraid, scared stiff in fact, of the laity and we do not want to allow them, in any way, shape or form, to share in any creative action in the Church. They are there just to listen and to obey. This will not do."

The Cardinal's secretary, a priest, was taking notes. He turned to the Cardinal at one point during my intervention and said, "The Bishops will not accept this."

Cardinal Cento just looked down at him and said, "It is a Bishop who is speaking."

***

I must confess that when I left for the Council in September 1962, I had no idea of what was to transpire. Like many others, I presumed that we would go to Rome, make some minor modifications to the Pre-Conciliar documents, approve them, then end up in a blaze of glory and come home. It is reliably reported that this was also the expectation of Pope John XXIII at the outset. Apparently he even wondered whether or not we should forego our pastoral obligations for Christmas that year and celebrate the closing of the Council in Rome on Christmas Day. This was not to be, however. The Council would not be over in one session, and it would take on a very surprising direction.

In his opening remarks to the Council, the Holy Father challenged the Bishops by calling for an "aggiornamento". He called us to see and examine the signs of the times. He spoke of our responsibility to explain our faith to the people and to live the life of the Church in the society of our day. He talked about being surrounded by prophets of doom rather than by people filled with hope. He reminded us that, although there could be no change in the substantial belief in the Divinity of Christ or in the Creed, which expresses the basic truths of our Church, there is a great difference between the way a truth is stated and the substance of that truth. There would always be room for deeper understanding. These truths could become more meaningful if expressed in the language of the day, using the images and the cultural developments of our time.

If the opening address of the Pope had not been enough, certainly our first meeting together further alerted us to the fact that this was not going to be a Council like the others. No one had been able to foresee the "crise de conscience" that would take place. Our soul searching would lead us to a profound examination of how we could best bring the life of Christ and the active presence of Christ to our people through the Church. We became acutely

Memoirs

aware of the need for the Church not only to re-examine its very nature and role but to examine our approach to the Council itself. With that, the Second Vatican Council began to take on a life of its own.

The Bishops of the world soon realized that this Council was going to be radically different from what any of us had anticipated. During our first meeting, a program which had been prepared in advance, was presented. Because this program did not meet the expectations of the Bishops, a motion was made to postpone the formal sessions of the Council for a few days. This would give the Conferences of Bishops from various continents and countries a chance to form new Commissions. They would be able to re-examine and, where necessary, change or rewrite the original proposals of the Pre-Conciliar Commissions. After some debate, it was agreed that we would adjourn. With this, the Bishops all stood and left the room. I was later informed that the Pope's secretary was looking out of his window and saw what was happening. He ran to the Pope's office in great excitement and said to the Holy Father, "All of the Bishops are leaving!" The Holy Father beamed and said, "Good! My Council begins!"

This brought about the first clash, if you can call it that, of two emerging groups in the Council - those who wanted little or no change, just some window-dressing, and those who wanted a very profound examination of the realities of our time.

Most of the Canadian Bishops, being in this latter group, were awakening to the fact that more time, thought and effort would have to be given to this Council. We realized that there would be more to the Council than just going in and giving speeches or listening to speeches. We knew we would have to do a lot of additional homework, much more studying, and also a great deal of praying!

It was clear that we had a responsibility not only to ourselves but to our people to become much more familiar with modern-day problems and current theological thought. Archbishop Philip Pocock was well advised, I think, when he suggested that we have a lecturer come in once a week while we were in Rome. He and I arranged with the Jesuits for the Canadian Bishops to use the hall in the Gregorian University. We invited all of the Canadian Bishops who wanted to come to hear interesting lectures from leading theologians and well-known Scripture scholars. We met every Sunday throughout the Council and it was an excellent series.

Attending lectures by men of the calibre of Cardinal Suenens, and listening to many other outstanding Bishops and distinguished theologians, with their vast knowledge of Theology, Canon Law or Scripture, gave one a new experience of Church. It was also a real education to meet with various groups of Bishops from around the world, including the Bishops of Africa, India, and East Asia. We knew theoretically that the Church was catholic and varied in colour and language. However, the lived

Memoirs

experience of listening to those Catholic Bishops from nations wherein the Catholic reality was just beginning to take root and blossom taught us a great deal. It was a "greening" of the European and Western Church.

***

What impressed me considerably as the Council progressed was the growing participation of the non-Catholic observers. The American Jesuit theologian, Gustave Weigel, who was responsible for advising the representatives of our sister Churches, did a magnificent job. Along with other advisors, he gave of himself unsparingly. He would sit up with them sometimes until two or three o'clock in the morning discussing the documents and the interventions. I think of him as one of the martyrs of the Council. He died of a heart attack very shortly thereafter. I think that many of Gus Weigel's colleagues would agree that he had surely worn himself out.

I was also impressed with the growing warmth and increasing interest shown by some of those observers who at first appeared rather aloof and suspicious and not very enthusiastic about the possibilities Vatican Council II might hold. By the second and third session of the Council their whole attitude had changed dramatically. I remember that during the discussion on the document on the Liturgy, there was a determined effort by some Bishops to try to defeat the original document, even though it had already been passed paragraph by paragraph. A number of the Bishops became worried that, when the time came to accept the document in its entirety, the final vote might actually go against it. I happened to be chatting at the coffee bar with two American Protestant theologians, Robert McAffy Brown of Berkeley, California and Albert Outler of the Southern Baptist Convention, who began to express their concern about these developments. They thought it was terrible that a small group would try to manipulate the Bishops on the final vote. They suggested that perhaps the Pope should be asked to intervene to postpone the vote until the situation could be resolved.

I replied, "We do not want the Pope to intervene. This will be a free vote and I do not have the slightest doubt that the result will be in our favour." Then I laughed and teasingly said to them, "You two Protestants, who do not even believe in the authority of the Pope, are probably the only ones in this room who would want to see the Pope intervene in this affair!" As it so happened, the document was far from being challenged in the final vote, and, as a matter of fact, was approved by a great majority.

It is interesting to note that, for each of the decrees passed by Vatican II, the number of votes were always overwhelmingly in favour. There can be no attention paid to anyone who says that these documents were pushed through by a stormy and powerful minority.

Memoirs

I must reiterate that this Council was a very democratic exercise. Anyone who wanted to participate had a chance to do so. Perhaps some of us might have intervened more than we did, but by the time the Cardinals were finished and a few more Bishops spoke, we usually had a clear indication of what the issue was and were satisfied that it had been sufficiently debated. Then we usually voted in favour of cutting off the discussion and going on to the next topic. At that point, those who still wished to make an intervention were invited to do so in writing.

I think this was a sensible procedure. Otherwise we would have been there forever. During the first session, when we were working on the document on the Liturgy, we had become bogged down in difficulties, disagreements and lack of consensus as we hammered out which changes should be made. The vernacular, for instance, was a bitter subject for many.

This brings to mind my mother's response. She was particularly furious with the change to the vernacular in the Liturgy because it had been her pride and joy for many years that she knew all the Latin answers. Whenever the Mass server did not appear on Sunday mornings when we were at our cottage at Fourteen Island Lake, she would love to sit in the front pew of the Church and answer the priest in Latin, to the great admiration of the surrounding congregation. When we would go to the door afterwards, the French-Canadian parishioners with whom she was always very close and with whom she liked to talk in her excellent French, would say, "T'es bien smart, Madame Carter. Tu sais tout ça." Mother saw her world being attacked as a result of the Council and she was not in very good humour when we came home.

In any event, the question of the change to the vernacular and several other major problems arose which justifiably had to be thoroughly debated, with pros and cons to be analyzed on both sides. A computer system had been installed for the Council, which was quite avant garde in those days. So, we went to the computer operators and asked them to calculate the length of time it would take to finish the Council if each of the documents of Vatican II were to be debated at the same rate as that of the Liturgy. In view of the number of discussions which were still to come and the number of decisions that had to be made, they told us it would take about thirty-eight years!

The only intervention I gave at the Council was during the debate on the document on the Laity. I had served on the Pre-Conciliar Commission and was not satisfied that our document, even in its revised state, was going far enough. I felt compelled to propose that we broaden the role of lay participation in the life and mission of the Church. So I gave my intervention, stating that I felt we could have done much better than we had. As a matter of fact, I stated that the chapter on the laity in the Council document: *The Constitution on the Church* (*Lumen*

Memoirs

Gentium) was far better than the document on the Laity from both a spiritual point of view and from the point of view of presenting a real challenge to our lay people. Apart from that intervention, like the rest of the Bishops, my role was to listen, to evaluate and to vote according to my conscience.

***

One of the saddest events which occurred during my Council days was the assassination of President John F. Kennedy on November 22, 1963. I have never forgotten the impact of this tragedy upon the people of Rome. My brother Emmett and I were out that evening and when we returned to our hotel, some of the Canadian Bishops were still in the restaurant. We joined them for a cup of coffee. A few minutes after we sat down, the head waiter came to our table looking very grave. He said, "Gentlemen, we have had terrible news and I thought you would like to know. Someone has shot John F. Kennedy, the President of the United States and he is very badly wounded." He left us in a state of shock as he returned to the kitchen, and we wondered how critical the condition of the President was and whether there was any chance for him to recover. In a few moments the maitre d' returned to our table and said, "I am very sorry to have to tell you this, but the President has just died." Deeply saddened, we left the restaurant.

The next day, I was amazed to see the effect that the news of the death of this foreign president had on the people of Rome. Men and women, and even young people, were walking about with tears in their eyes. It was almost as if their own president, or someone they had known and loved very much, had died. That memory is still vivid after so many years.

***

As the Council continued, two disturbing events occurred. The first was at the beginning of the third session in September 1964, when we were studying a statement concerning the Jewish people. There was a very nasty underhanded attempt to influence the Bishops. Anonymous papers were distributed from an unknown source and some of them contained material that was actually vicious. It breathed hatred. Whoever was behind that subversive movement even had the nerve to distribute the Protocols of the Wise Men of Zion (imagine!) to Bishops who are supposed to be intelligent men - at least intelligent and judicious enough to know that these had been pronounced forgeries by experts years earlier. It was a distressing experience.

The second incident was what appeared to be an effort to try to stop the document on freedom of conscience, the *Declaration on Religious Liberty*. That one also blew up in the third session. Bishop de Smedt of Bruges, who was the reporter, read the prologue and brought the substance of the document to our attention. Then, after some days of discussion, the Secretary General of the Council, Archbishop Pericle Felici, got up and announced in his superb Latin that this document had been withdrawn from further discussion. Some of us were alarmed enough to get together and have a meeting immediately. We decided that we had to do something about this. We went to Cardinal Meyer of Chicago, one of four Cardinals who presided at the sessions. We pointed out to him that, if this document was withdrawn, the American Bishops would have to do a great deal of explaining to their people when they returned home. Everyone was under the impression that this document would be seriously discussed. Since it was regarded as a very important document, the Bishops felt that we had to express our strong objection to this action. Some of the American Bishops suggested that we distribute a petition for the Bishops to sign requesting that the freedom of conscience document be brought back on the floor.

When they started to write the petition by hand, I said, "You will never get enough copies ready and distributed in time. We have twenty-five hundred Bishops here. Maybe we could have copies run off."

There was a young American seminarian standing nearby who said, "They do printing in Felici's office behind the sacristy. All the documents are being turned out there. Someone should go in and ask them to run off your petition."

I volunteered saying, "I think I know enough Italian to tell them what we want done." So I followed the seminarian into the office and I spoke to the layman who was in charge.

"Could we have this paper run off here?" I asked.

"Oh, si, Monsignori, certainly. How many copies do you want?"

I told him we needed enough to distribute to the Council Fathers. So he ran them off and gave them to us.

Then I said to the seminarian, "Now look. Don't get yourself into any trouble. That was Felici's office. He is going to be furious when he finds out. So in case you are asked who was with you, I am not telling you my name. You can simply say it was a Bishop, but you do not know who he was. If they want to know where he was from, just say he was an English-speaking Bishop and that is all. Don't stick your neck out."

The petition was distributed and the next day a statement was made by Pope Paul VI assuring us that the freedom of conscience document would be the first one on the docket at the next session.

The following year I was in my seat at the Council and a young man came over to me and said, "Do you remember me?"

"Yes, you are the seminarian who brought me to the printing room in Felici's office."

Then he told me about the following conversation he had had with his Superior:

"The Rector said to me, 'You brought a Bishop into Felici's printing office during the last session of Vatican II.'

'Yes, Monsignor. I did.'

'Well, I have had a complaint about you for having done that. Now, who was that Bishop?'

'I do not know who the Bishop was.'

'Surely you must know!'

'No, there were several Bishops there and one of them asked me if I would take him into the office where he could have a paper run off. He was English-speaking. I took him into the office. And that is all I know.'

'Well, they think you should be punished for what you did.'"

"The Monsignor then looked at me very severely and said, 'You actually brought an English-speaking Bishop into Felici's office to run off the petition that the *Declaration on Religious Liberty* be brought back for discussion at the Council?'

'Yes, Monsignor, I did.'

"And with that, the Monsignor leaned back in his chair and began to laugh. 'Well', he said, 'That is a good one. Go back to your room and forget about it.'"

I thought this little anecdote could be told now. I have never mentioned it publicly before. It certainly has a humorous side when compared with the seriousness of the Council. I often wonder whatever became of that seminarian.

***

Another little anecdote I remember concerns the thoughtfulness and generosity of Pope Paul VI. It was during the second session of the Council in 1963. All of the Canadian Bishops were being received by the new Pope who had just been elected in June of that year. Cardinal Léger was making the introductions and Emmett and I happened to be standing together.

The Cardinal said, as we approached, "These two Bishops are brothers. Their dear mother is almost ninety years of age."

The Holy Father said, "Oh, I must send her a rosary."

He turned to one of his attendants and asked him to go and get a nice rosary. So the lad trotted off. He had to walk almost half a mile, I suppose, to get to the Pope's office in the Vatican. By the time he returned, the Pope was just finishing speaking to us. The attendant came over, bringing the rosary to him.

The Pope looked at it and said, "Oh no, no, no - non questo - not this one. I want the mother-of-pearl rosary, the best. It is for the mother of two Bishops."

So the poor fellow had to trot back all that way again. When he finally returned, the Pope came over to us and gave us a beautiful mother-of-pearl rosary.

Mother was confined to bed at that time because of a fall in which she had broken her back. When we returned to Montreal we gave her the rosary from Pope Paul VI. She was very grateful and so thrilled that she wrote to the Holy Father with that beautiful script of hers. She told him how happy she was to have been singled out by him for this recognition and this beautiful present.

The following Christmas the Pope decided to send all the Bishops of the world a cake and some Italian caramels. It was a vast undertaking. This gesture was typical of Paul VI who liked to show his fraternal affection for the Bishops. Emmett and I each received a package about a week or so before Christmas.

When I went home for my annual Christmas visit that I would make around the sixth of January, I brought the goodies to Mother and said, "Here is a present from the Holy Father."

Well, of course, her eyes lit up. She opened up the package and saw the caramels and the cake and said, "He must have received my letter. I will have to write to him again and thank him."

Alex Carter

All I could say to Mother was, "Yes, that would be nice," and then I went to my sister Margaret and said, "For heaven's sake, you had better intercept any letter that Mother writes to the Pope. I simply said that the present was from the Holy Father and she drew her own conclusion. She thinks that he sent *her* the cake and caramels. Whoever opens the mail in the Pope's office might be a little puzzled if they see a letter from some Canadian lady thanking the Holy Father for the caramels and cake he sent her for Christmas." I said, "I would not want to have someone making inquiries as to who this woman is and what this was all about." So the little thank you letter that Mother wrote to the Holy Father was never mailed.

***

While we were attending the Council, I knew we had an obligation to keep our priests and people at home well-informed on all the major issues and developments that were emerging. I believe that many Bishops acquired a richer vision of their role in the Church during that Council. Some moved from an old text-book type of theology to a much more challenging and much more profound theology. The danger, of course, was that, while our own attitudes were changing, we might forget that our priests and our people, enlightened only by a few articles in newspapers, knew little or nothing about what was taking place in Rome.

I was well aware of this because of my own mother's reaction to the Council. After each session,

Memoirs

when my brother and I would go to visit Mother, we would be criticized greatly for any change that she did not like. She showed complete contempt for the achievement of the Bishops at the first session of the Council. She suggested that the only thing we had accomplished was to add St. Joseph's name to the Canon of the Mass. "It was hardly worthwhile to bring all the Bishops of the world to Rome just for that," she said.

When I returned to the Diocese at the end of each session, my first priority was to meet with the priests and report to them. I tried to summarize the developments of Vatican II as objectively as possible. I shared with them the various points of view of the Council on how we could best keep the faith alive and make it more meaningful and challenging to our people in this day and age. As pastors, they were going to have to cope with the changes in society, the new structure of society, and the various breakthroughs in cultural, intellectual and scientific circles. These meetings with the priests were always pleasant for me.

My second major concern was to involve the lay people in this education process. I thought it would be well advised to gather representative lay people from across the Diocese following each session of the Council. We would give them summaries of the documents that had been or were being discussed and invite them to participate in discussions and share their reactions, their feelings and their understanding of what was taking place. This was the beginning of what we called the "Little Council". Some two hundred delegates and most of our priests from across the Diocese met in Sudbury to debate new orientations and new directions. Our French-speaking and English-speaking groups met separately and the sessions closed with a short joint meeting, followed by a Liturgical celebration.

I believe the "Little Council" helped us all a great deal. It made the transition to a Post-Conciliar Church, with the drastic changes entailed, more easily acceptable. Obviously not everyone was in total agreement. Some resented particular changes. Others wanted more revolutionary ones. But, on the whole, I felt that the majority of our priests and people certainly responded very well.

News of our "Little Council" spread to the United States. I received letters from a few American Bishops, including the Cardinal of St. Louis, asking for information. I answered them saying, "By all means I can tell you how we organized the "Little Council", but I am sure that, given the size of your Diocese and the vast resources available to you, you could do a much better job. Certainly our basic plan could be revised and adapted to your own situation. If it is of any value to you, I am delighted to share it with you." I just mention this in passing because it is part of my own experience of the good spirit that existed among the Bishops at the Council.

***

During the third session of the Council, with the continuing demands made upon me by the Diocese, and with the additional tasks being handed

Memoirs

to me by the Conference of Canadian Bishops, I thought it was time to ask for an Auxiliary. It was all the more necessary because I felt the time had come to give more reassurance to the Francophone population by having a French-speaking Auxiliary. That had always been my intention. However, one had to create an atmosphere, or at least work toward a change in atmosphere, before going ahead with what could be a bone of contention in part of the Diocese. By this time, I even had someone in mind for the position. I had known this man and watched him work and pray. I saw his great devotion to the Church and his goodness. I had pretty well decided that this was the type of Auxiliary Bishop who would be right for our Diocese. I am talking about Adolphe Proulx. I made my request to Rome in 1964 through Archbishop Sergio Pignedoli, who had just recently become the Delegate to Canada. As always, he received me very cordially in Ottawa and, after listening attentively to the reasons I outlined, he said that we would begin the process immediately. As well as Adolphe, I had to submit two other names, which presented no difficulty. By that time I had met many fine priests, not only around Montreal, but particularly through my work at the Canadian Conference of Bishops and its various Commissions. But Adolphe was the one I wanted as my French-speaking Auxiliary.

I heard nothing from the Delegate for a while but I knew that the process would take time. Later on he asked me to come to see him. I could tell from our conversation that he had run into some opposition to my request. At our meeting, he asked me if I realized that I was creating a precedent in Canada, pointing out that there was no record of an English-speaking Bishop with a French-speaking Auxiliary in any diocese in the country.

So I said to him, "Frankly, I was not aware that this was something new. However, I believe that it would be good for our Diocese to have a French-speaking Auxiliary. If this creates a precedent, maybe it is time for a precedent to be created. This is a matter of justice. It is a matter of recognizing that in our Diocese we have two main language groups, almost equal in number, each group having its own traditions. They have their own needs, liturgically and otherwise. Even the mentality is different between the French-speaking Catholics and the English-speaking Catholics of this Diocese. They come from different backgrounds. There are not too many dioceses in Canada like Sault Ste. Marie."

He did not argue any further. He seemed to be satisfied. I heard no more until I was notified that Adolphe Proulx had been called to the Episcopate. Pignedoli left it to me to inform him. I telephoned Adolphe and asked him to come to see me as soon as possible.

He came that afternoon. We sat and chatted for a few minutes and I said, "I have some news for you, Adolphe." He suddenly became more attentive.

"I have decided that I need an Auxiliary in this Diocese. I looked around, considered several names, and decided that you were the one who could do the job. I made my request to the Holy See and I have just received word from the Apostolic Delegate that you are going to be the Auxiliary Bishop of Sault Ste. Marie."

Being such a humble man, Adolphe responded by giving me all the reasons why he was not a good choice and why I should change the appointment. I still recall our conversation that day with a certain amount of humour and pleasure. Obviously I disagreed with him. I consecrated Adolphe Proulx a Bishop at the Pro-Cathedral in North Bay in February 1965.

I realize that this appointment came as a great surprise to many people. I am sure that, in general, it met with the approval of the majority of the priests. It certainly brought reassurance to the French-Canadian community, the assurance that they were not going to be treated as a small and unimportant minority. They were to have a full share in the life of the Church, a Church which would be better able to meet the religious needs of their people in the Diocese. I would just like to say that Adolphe more than fulfilled my hopes as a loyal and devoted French-Canadian Auxiliary.

When I came to the Sault Diocese, it was a new experience for me to have contact with the different Franco-Ontarian associations such as l'Association canadienne-française de l'Ontario (ACFO). Sudbury had become quite an important centre in the whole of the Franco-Ontarian society. At the same time, Radio Canada (the French National Radio and Television Network) was beginning to take a greater interest in our bilingual Diocese. I was particularly grateful to Bishop Proulx for being my liaison with these different groups.

I could never, for one moment, regret my decision; first, to have a French-speaking Auxiliary; and secondly, to have chosen Bishop Proulx. I thought I would have him with me for many years. Unfortunately, fate intervened. A few years later, the Bishop of the Diocese of Alexandria was transferred and the See became vacant. This created a sequence of events which are curious enough to mention.

I wrote to Archbishop Pignedoli, the Apostolic Delegate, and told him I thought that some Bishops would probably suggest the transfer of Bishop Proulx to Alexandria, but that, in my opinion, this would not be a wise move. The large number of people Adolphe was serving as my Francophone Auxiliary exceeded the population of the Diocese of Alexandria. I was certain it would be much easier to find another Bishop for Alexandria than to replace Bishop Proulx in our Diocese.

I heard no more. Everything was going along very smoothly. After a meeting in Ottawa, I spent a day or two at our family home in Montreal. I was just preparing to return to North Bay when I received a call from the Apostolic Delegation. It was the Chargé d'Affaires because Pignedoli was in

Memoirs

Rome. He asked to see me, saying that it was of utmost importance. I said, "I am not planning to stop in Ottawa on my way to North Bay. I am flying directly from here. If you want to come to Montreal this afternoon, I can meet you at my family home," and I gave him the address. When he arrived he told me that he had received an urgent message from Archbishop Pignedoli in Rome, asking him to see me to explain the circumstances surrounding the situation in Alexandria.

He informed me that there had been a long delay in naming a Bishop to Alexandria and during the interim, an ecclesiastical rumour had begun to circulate that the Diocese was going to be closed and divided between Kingston and Ottawa. This had caused a great deal of uproar and anger in Alexandria. Delegations had been sent to Archbishop Pignedoli and there were protests right across the Diocese. Finally a Bishop from another diocese in Canada had been offered the appointment and had accepted. The announcement was to be made very shortly. Since there had been such a long delay, and because of all the rumours, the Holy See was very anxious that the new Bishop be installed as soon as possible. Unfortunately, Pignedoli had just learned that this Bishop had changed his mind and no longer wanted to go to Alexandria. This really upset the applecart.

"Now", he said, "Archbishop Pignedoli is asking if you would remove your veto on the appointment of Bishop Proulx to Alexandria."

I was very surprised and amazed that he would ask me to "remove my veto". I thought I had simply made a request or a recommendation. So I answered, "We are all at the service of the Church. If that is the situation, and if the only sensible solution right now is to have Bishop Proulx go to Alexandria, I certainly will not stand in the way. I wish this had not happened but if the situation is going to cause difficulty for the Church, then we will all have to adapt to the circumstances. As much as I will hate to see him go, I also know that they will be getting a fine Bishop. Tell the Archbishop to proceed with the necessary arrangements and I will start looking for another French-speaking Auxiliary."

***

I have aged, if not grown wise, in the service of the Church and I deeply believe that I only really learned the true and full nature of that Church during the dramatic, exciting and challenging years between 1962 and 1965. Those were the years - the time of Vatican II - during which I lived a traumatic experience. It involved joy, fear, wonderment, anxiety and Heaven knows how many other emotions that people experience when they are challenged by the Spirit to accept a conversion that radically changes their point of view on matters that substantially influence their whole life. Those were the years during which all of the Bishops faced the immense challenges that the Council brought to them personally as well as to the Church.

Memoirs

Vatican II ended in the fall of 1965 on a note of harmony and reconciliation, of mutual love and commitment. I will never forget the last day of business and the Mass that was offered by Pope Paul VI. He concelebrated (concelebration had now become a reality) not only with the Bishops, but also with theologians who had been our advisors during the Council. Many of these outstanding theologians had helped us immensely over the years to keep up with the theology of our times: Congar, Chenu, de Lubac, Danielou, Ratzinger, Kung, Rahner, Schillebeeckx and many more. Their thinking was vital to the development of the Church. Some of the theologians present at the Mass had previously been forbidden to publish by the Holy Office, but their names had now been cleared and they were there with Pope Paul VI. I think this was a great tribute to the Pope. It was a beautiful act of recognition and gratitude and, for some who might have been unjustly treated, perhaps a sign of atonement. The great unity between the Holy Father and the theologians of the Council is an example that we should remember and for which we should be grateful.

The Post-Conciliar Years

Towards the end of 1964, the Canadian Bishops held their annual meeting, for the last time, in Rome. We knew we had to look forward to the future of our Conference and plan for the time when the Council would be over. When it came time for the election of the General Secretaries, Cardinal Léger took most of the Bishops by surprise by asking that the Secretaries be excused. The usual procedure was for someone simply to move that the Secretaries be engaged for the following year and everyone would raise their hand to approve the nominations. The Cardinal's request indicated that we were dealing with something more serious this time. He said, and rightly so, that the Council was going to bring great and important changes in our Conference. He felt that we needed full-time, not part-time, General Secretaries. Speaking for the French sector, he suggested that we express our gratitude to Monseigneur Raymond Limoges for his contribution and engage a man full-time who would help us implement the teachings of Vatican

II. The man's name was Father Charles Mathieu, a very clever and experienced sociologist in Montreal. There were no objections to this.

After the meeting, however, a few of the Bishops in the English sector were discussing the issue and realized that we, too, would need a full-time General Secretary, someone comparable to a man as outstanding and imposing as Charles Mathieu. I suggested Father Gordon George who had recently finished his term as Provincial of the English-speaking Canadian Jesuits. He was a sociologist as well and would be a good counterpart to Father Mathieu. Archbishop Pocock was very much in favour so we decided to get in touch with him.

At first Father George was not particularly interested because the idea of the Secretary's job did not appeal to him. However, when he learned that the implementation of Vatican II would be done partly on a national basis and through the Bishops' Conference, he became very interested. I suggested he fly over to Rome to meet with us. When he arrived we explained that we needed a full-time man who could help the Bishops face the implementation of the Council and that it was not going to be an easy task. It would call for much study and would involve the whole gamut of Church life: education, catechetics, Liturgy and the social obligations that would arise from the Pastoral Constitution on *The Church in the Modern World* (*Gaudium et Spes*).

Memoirs

So we gave our thanks to Monsignor John Carley who had served the smaller and more limited Conference so well on a part-time basis, and Father George took over as the English-speaking General Secretary. We now had two men who were well-equipped to face the challenges of the future and who proved invaluable to the Canadian Bishops as they set about their task at the end of the Council.

***

I am sure that all the Bishops who were at Vatican II returned home realizing that their work was cut out for them. We could not continue to function as though nothing had happened. There was much to do and many vital changes to be made. We knew we would be fully occupied in trying to bring the message of Vatican II to our people. We would also have to try to explain to them the reasons for the great changes that needed to be made.

The first thing the Canadian Bishops decided to do was to reorganize the Conference. We wanted to bring it more in line with the collegial teaching of *Lumen Gentium*. Until this time, the President of the Canadian Conference of Bishops was elected, not by all of the Bishops of Canada, but by a Board. The Board was a small group composed of the Cardinals and a few Bishops, mostly Archbishops. There was nothing wrong with that. It was the way things were done and no one complained. But after

Alex Carter

Vatican II, a Commission was established to study the structure of the CCC, and I was named by the Conference to be Co-Chairman of that Commission. We were to present our recommendations at the next general meeting of the Conference.

When we made our report, the first item on the agenda was the election of the President. Naturally, it had been the custom that alternately there would be a Francophone and an Anglophone Bishop elected to that position and we recommended that this not be changed. However, the Commission thought it would be a better expression of collegiality if the President of the Conference were to be elected by all of the Bishops instead of by the Board. Speaking on behalf of our Commission, I proposed that, beginning the following year, this new procedure be adopted. Several of us on the Commission had worked on this question and we had not really anticipated any difficulty or any opposition, though probably we should have. To my great surprise, the man who actually spoke in opposition to this was Cardinal Léger. Of course, one must remember that Léger exercised a great deal of influence with the members of the Board and could play a major part in the choice of President.

In response, as Co-Chairman of the Commission, I reiterated that we thought it would be much more democratic and much more in line with the collegial teaching of the Council for the President to be chosen by his colleagues. It finally came to a vote and was passed by a large majority.

Cardinal Léger still had some real concerns which he expressed to me during the coffee break. He told me he feared that the Bishops might elect someone who lacked the necessary qualities to be President. I said that I had more confidence than that in the Canadian Bishops and I thought they were quite capable of electing a good leader. During our discussion I told him I found it strange that he was not in agreement with us because he was always such a leader in the Council discussions on the collegial aspect of the Bishops of the Church. I said that a democratic election seemed to be more in keeping with that spirit and with that teaching.

The Cardinal was very unhappy. I do not think he ever quite reconciled himself to that decision. As I look back on that meeting, I still believe that we did the right thing. I think that our Conference would not have succeeded or developed the way it did had not this more democratic and collegial procedure been voted in. The only problem, and for me personally it was a great problem, was that when we had the vote, the Bishops elected me President. At that point I wondered whether or not Cardinal Léger's fears might not have been justified!

Prior to this I had consented, with great reservations, to accept the position of Treasurer of the CCC. Archbishop Marie-Joseph Lemieux of Ottawa, who had been the Treasurer, had relinquished the office. Before leaving, he had warned me of the possible danger that we were facing. We would be running a deficit in the CCC if we continued to operate as we had. This was particularly true if we were to undertake some of the projects under discussion, such as increasing the Offices and Commissions. We were entering a time of serious decision-making. I knew I would have to ask the Bishops to increase their financial contributions to the CCC. Anyone who has ever had to ask for more money knows it is never an easy task. We simply had to bite the bullet. We were obliged to raise the per capita significantly, particularly in the English sector. When I was suddenly projected into the President's chair, I did not feel that I should give the Treasurer's work to anyone else under those circumstances. With everyone's agreement, I was to stay on as Treasurer for about six months until we could reorganize the department. We would then elect a Treasurer who would be able to take over the challenging duties of the office.

Just as a matter of interest, when we opened our General Assembly for the first time to the Press, the correspondents, who were sitting at the back of the room, were very anxious to get a look at our financial report. We had a table up front on which I had placed a number of bound copies of our Treasurer's report for the previous year and these were made available to them. The correspondents made a rush to consult the report to find out how much money we had. When they saw our meagre resources they quickly lost interest.

One of the most trying times for most of the Canadian Bishops was our Conference meeting in

Memoirs

Winnipeg - St. Boniface in 1968. At that time we were discussing the Holy Father's encyclical letter, *Humanae Vitae.* He was dealing with the sacredness and dignity of human life, as well as the issue of birth control. The Canadian Bishops, after lengthy debate, prepared a statement for their people, a copy of which they sent to the Holy Father. They expressed their solidarity with him but raised some critical questions about the pastoral application of *Humanae Vitae* to the many complex situations which existed among faithful Catholics in this country.

The Bishops' statement brought mixed reactions in the weeks and months that followed our meeting. Though many praised it, it caused some scandal and a great deal of distress to others. Our position was attacked by writers who claimed that we had opposed the Holy Father and had rejected the Encyclical. Fortunately we had received a letter from the Secretary of State of the Vatican saying that the Holy Father had read our statement on *Humanae Vitae* "with satisfaction". As President of the CCC, I had received that letter from the Apostolic Delegate in Ottawa which was dated October 21, 1968 and read:

Your Excellency,

This Apostolic Delegation promptly transmitted to the Holy See a copy of the declaration made by the Bishops of Canada during their general assembly at Saint Boniface on the Encyclical Letter "Humanae Vitae".

Alex Carter

Now I am happy to notify Your Excellency that His Eminence, Amleto Cardinal Cicognani, Secretary of State to His Holiness, has just communicated to the Delegation that the Holy Father, Pope Paul VI, has taken cognisance of the document with satisfaction.

With every best wish, I am

Sincerely yours in Our Lord,
+ E.Clarizio
Apostolic Delegate

After the Winnipeg meeting, when it was announced that we had received this message from the Holy Father, I was beseiged by reporters and others. They were taking issue with the phrase "with satisfaction" and wanted to know what it meant. I simply said to them, "Well, you know the meaning of the word 'satisfaction' as well as I do. It does not mean 'joy and exultation'; it does not mean 'displeasure and regret'. If you are 'satisfied', you are 'satisfied'. The Holy Father was 'satisfied' with our statement. That was all we asked for and all we hoped for. That letter should have put an end to any questioning or any doubts. However, some people will never accept the truth if it does not please them.

***

During the Post-Conciliar period we began to open new avenues in our attempt to carry out some

Memoirs

of the principles enunciated by the Council. One area that received a good deal of attention was that of Ecumenism. This was due in large measure to the efforts of Cardinal Leo Joseph Suenens of Brussels-Malines (Mechlin), that very fine churchman who was an enthusiastic and effective promoter of Ecumenism. He had a special relationship with the Church of England. The Archbishop of Canterbury, Michael Ramsey, and he became great friends. In fact, they went to the United States together preaching a series of retreats to the various members and priests of the Episcopalian Church.

Closer to home, in our own Diocese, we had made great efforts to improve relations with our sister Christian Churches. I had a very cordial visit with Archbishop Ramsey when I attended the Anglican Synod in the city of Sault Ste. Marie. At the beginning of the liturgical celebration which opened the Synod in St. Luke's Anglican Cathedral in the Sault, I was placed right in front of Archbishop Ramsey in the procession. He was walking with Archbishop William Wright, the Anglican Archbishop of Algoma. I looked around and saw many of our Sisters of St. Joseph there and numerous people that I recognized from our own Cathedral parish. I turned to Archbishop Wright and said, "You know, I think there are more of my people here than there are of yours." Ramsey laughed and Wright said, "I would not be surprised if you were right."

***

Alex Carter

We also tried to redeem the promise that we had made ourselves at the beginning of Vatican II to give preferential consideration to the needs of the poor. We had a very obvious example right in our own Diocese. The Native People, who had experienced so much poverty, were just beginning the struggle to revitalize their own culture. We were very fortunate in the past to have had the Jesuit Fathers who had given so much of themselves to our Native People. There were many beautiful stories and examples of their dedication. However, I realized that, with the changing nature of our society and our world, the Church would have to go beyond the kind of evangelization which had been the focus until then and allow the Native People to appreciate and develop their own culture.

In the spring of 1962, Father Gordon George, the Superior of the Jesuits who were working with our Native People, offered to send Father Dan Hannin to take a degree in sociology. This would enable Dan to further the work he had already begun in the Native communities through the Legion of Mary. We hoped that on his return he would be able to promote and help develop the social education of our Native People, with the intention of forming leaders among them - leaders who would go on to play a significant role in the spiritual renewal of their own people. After Father Hannin returned in 1964, I asked the Jesuits whether Dan could also act as the Coordinator of our Diocesan Synod, for which preparations were to begin in 1966. I felt that the Diocesan Synod would also benefit the Native Peoples by enabling them to begin to be recognized as a separate body, belonging to our Church, but with their own needs, their own culture and their own spirituality. This could certainly be realized without endangering the unity of the Church.

As a matter of fact, one of the lessons learned during the Second Vatican Council was that we had to recognize the local cultures of the various nations if we hoped to see them becoming more involved in the Church. The rightness and the propriety of this decision has been borne out by the fact that the Church has flourished among the black nations of Africa. The inculturation process encourages black Christian people to keep their own identity and express themselves in their own way, according to their own customs, as they embrace the teachings of the Church.

There is no doubt at all in my mind that the move away from total uniformity was one of the greatest achievements of the Council. The Church realizes more than ever that there can be unity among people of different mentalities who come from different backgrounds. What is important is that our convictions be basically the same - that the truth we believe and the God we serve are equally the object of our love and affection.

***

Alex Carter

During these early Post-Conciliar years, the Bishops of Canada saw a need to update the teaching of religion in our schools. In the CCC we gave serious attention to the Canadian Catechism. We made arrangements with the Quebec Bishops, who had already started their own Catechism, to adapt it to the needs of the young people and the teachers in the English-speaking schools.

I know that there are many people who are negative in their criticism of the Canadian Catechism. I know that there is a difference of opinion concerning what happened in the development of our religious instruction of children. I suppose, like everything else, it was a new and a radical attempt at change. Like most such attempts, it had its weaknesses. Perhaps we did with that undertaking what we did with the Liturgy - we went a little too fast for the proper assimilation of the new directions. It should come as no surprise that a completely new approach to catechetics would cause great difficulties.

At the same time, one must admit, that where the effort was properly made, the new Catechism was effective. It was not nearly such a disaster as some of the prophets of doom tell us today. Where it did not succeed, I am not convinced that it was entirely the fault of the new Catechism. I believe that the fault was often in the "trahison des clercs". Because it was new, different, and challenging, many priests just stopped teaching religion. They were more at home with the *Butler* or *Baltimore*

Catechisms than they were with something that was built upon a new approach. Many of our Catholic parents, and some of our teachers, had a similar reaction. They were satisfied with the simple question and answer method of instructing the children. They resented very much a new Catechism which did not speak their language completely and simply. I also believe that we had allowed our Catholic parents to become indifferent to the teaching of religion to their children in the home. I do not believe it is the school's role to be the first to teach children to make the Sign of the Cross or to say the *Our Father* or *Hail Mary*. Children should have learned those prayers as surely and as quickly as they learned to talk. If we Catholics believe what we profess, we should not be sitting back waiting for catechism to be taught only in the school. The teaching of religion requires support from a faith-filled home.

At the time, I thought that it would take about twenty-five years for an objective and proper appreciation to be given to those who devoted so much time and thought to the new Catechism. Despite its failings, it had great appeal and its approach was probably much more fruitful in the long-run than simply learning by rote. The development of a catechism as an effective instrument of teaching religion has to be an on-going process. Our society is changing so fast now and many of these changes are so substantive that we will simply have to be continually updating it. In fact, we have already been through several rewritings of the Canadian Catechism. As a dispassionate observer, I still feel that the change was well-conceived and well-founded. I am convinced that it did a lot of good. If some Solomon could prove what should have been done, instead of what was done, it would be interesting to know his conclusions. Unfortunately we do not have the power or the ability to go back and do a comparative study to determine which approach would have been better.

***

As the Church was re-examining herself, inspired by the two basic documents of the Council: *The Constitution on the Church* (*Lumen Gentium*) and *The Church in the Modern World* (*Gaudium et Spes*), She was faced with great difficulties. There were two diverse mentalities; one favoured collegiality, the other favoured central control - the concept of community versus that of organized conformity. Face to face, you had one group which insisted upon uniformity as the most essential element, and another group which wanted to foster an acceptable and realistic pluralism in the Church. The latter were not suggesting a pluralism of doctrine or revealed Truth - rather a pluralism of ways of expressing these truths. With the existence of these two different approaches, confrontation was inevitable at every level, including the universal Church and the local Church.

We had seen this type of confrontation at the universal level between the members of the Curia and the Bishops who were the representatives of

Memoirs

their Conferences at the Extraordinary Synod of 1971. The role of the Bishop as head of his diocesan Church was conceived by most of the delegates to the Synod to be in keeping with the teaching and the concept of the Church as found in *Lumen Gentium*. The role of the Bishop as we saw it was given in Chapter Three of that document. However, for some who were in authority at the centre of the Church, the Roman Curia, there was a different point of view. They were still inclined to stress central control.

It was also quite easy to discern these differences of opinion among the members of our local Church. We had experienced them during our "Little Council" and the Diocesan Synod in 1966, as we started to reflect upon the need to restructure our diocesan life and some of its organizational forms. I will cite only one example. We saw it in our attempt to build up parish councils. Our desire to give real responsibility to those people who had the ability and the desire to serve naturally pleased some of our priests and people very much, while others were frightened and very much opposed to the idea. It was not always an easy task to bring everyone into at least a general acceptance of the way we were trying to carry out Vatican II and make it a living reality in our Diocese.

***

On Social issues we knew that adapting our local Churches and our national Churches to the teachings of Vatican II was not going to be easy. We were trying to answer the Encyclical Letters of the Holy Fathers, particularly John XXIII and Paul VI. One of our goals was to mobilize our people to help the Third World nations. The Canadian Catholic Organization for Development and Peace (CCODP) was launched in 1967, just two years after the Council had ended, and I think it has proven itself to be one of our better accomplishments. We tried to answer the Holy Father's request, not only to bring food to the developing countries of the Third World, but more importantly, to help them help themselves, which is their greatest need. That is why CCODP was conceived and what it is all about. There were moments when we were a little worried about the trends that some were trying to introduce into the Organization. However, with wisdom, proper dialogue and action on the part of those responsible for the Organization, we were able to keep it growing in the right direction. On the whole, we can certainly say that they tried to fulfill the mandate that they received and are remaining faithful to the character that we wanted to give to the CCODP.

In justice, we have to pay a great tribute to the Canadian government for helping this Church organization. Through CIDA they matched our funds, dollar for dollar, to enable us to do twice as much as we would have been able to do on our own. As a matter of fact, I have been told by some very influential people in the Canadian government that they were delighted to be able to do this. They felt that we could do more to help the poor than the government could do directly, and with less administrative expense.

***

One of our ideas which did not come to fruition was that of having a National Laity Council. We wanted to form a representative group of laity from across Canada who would become advisors to the Bishops as they faced the challenges of bringing about change in the fields of social doctrine, education and other areas of concern within the Church. It was our hope that this group would work together to formulate a plan of action that would help us fulfill what we considered to be our duty according to the teachings of Vatican Council II. The concept was good. The problem was the complexity of our society.

As I look back on it, I still think we made a noble attempt. We did bring together a group of lay people who met with representatives from the Conference of Bishops. I think it was my brother Emmett and Archbishop Aurèle Plourde of Ottawa who were designated by the Conference to work with the Catholic laity to establish this Council. After two or three meetings, however, it appeared that there was no way of reaching a consensus. I think the size of our country and the diversity among Canadian Catholics probably made the task more difficult than it would have been under different circumstances.

Because of such difficulties and complexities, we were not too surprised to see this endeavour given a very polite, friendly and noble Christian burial at the General Assembly of the CCC that year. I do not think our efforts were wasted, however, because the ideas that germinated probably did some good at the provincial level or at the local level for Church members. The very fact that we were not able to have a National Laity Council may have led to more initiative on the part of local groups who believed in lay action and who believed in the baptismal character of the individual Catholic.

***

The time came when we had to prepare for the 1971 Synod. I must say that the Canadian Bishops always took the Synods seriously. We held meetings and had theologians helping us to prepare. We had extensive consultations among our priests and people across the country. The staff at the CCC was always given the task of preparing documents and discussion papers for the Bishops. All of this enabled us to speak as a group with some unity and coherence as we brought our thoughts and opinions to the various Synods. 1971 was no exception. I remember that our General Secretaries and the Heads of Departments of the CCC worked extremely hard, some of them even to the point of exhaustion, as they helped us prepare for the two major topics of the Synod: The Ministry of the Priesthood and Social Justice.

Memoirs

I had been chosen as one of the delegates, along with Archbishops Aurèle Plourde of Ottawa and Paul Grégoire of Montreal, and Cardinal George Flahiff of Winnipeg. Once again we found ourselves addressing some basic questions. While the Synod was to be primarily concerned with the Ministry of the Priesthood and Social Justice, it also included issues which had been discussed during the Council and afterwards, in the various hierarchies - particularly in France, Ireland, Switzerland and parts of Germany.

***

Some of us were already "marked men" due to the 1969 Synod and the topic of Collegiality, on which I had made an intervention on behalf of the Canadian Bishops. Also during that Synod, Cardinal Suenens had invited me to meet with him, Cardinal Alfrink of Utrecht, Cardinal Doepfner of Munich and two or three others to prepare a presentation asking for the reform of the Curia. The idea was that the Bishops would take over their legitimate task as the legislative body under and with the Holy Father. The Curia would take on the duty of a Secretariat which would carry out the wishes of the Holy Father and the College of Bishops, and their Synodal decisions.

We tried hard to have what we considered a much more theological approach restored to the Church. We did not succeed, however, nor was the Curia enthused with our proposal, but at least we were able to make the Pope aware of the fact that the Bishops would like to be consulted and that the Synod was an instrument which could facilitate such consultations.

***

Getting back to the 1971 Synod, I cannot say that the Canadian Bishops were able to impress everyone with our reasoning. Sometimes, I am afraid, we caused some annoyance and maybe some pain in our attempts to be objective. On the first topic, the Priesthood, we had taken surveys in Canada, and as part of my report I presented the results of those surveys. I could sense that my intervention on celibacy was causing real anxiety and pain to the Holy Father. He was sitting not far from me and I could read the expression on his face. We did not consider ourselves to be revolutionaries, but I reported that, in our surveys, we found that the majority of the priests of Canada felt that the Conferences should be given the right to determine the possibility of ordaining married men, if that would better respond to the needs of the Church and the people. We felt that this was a perfectly logical issue to be discussed, but knowing the reaction that would come, it was somewhat painful for me to have to present that paper on behalf of the Canadian Bishops.

Our suggestion, of course, came as a bombshell to many. As we were leaving the hall at the close of the session I found myself next to an American

Bishop who turned to me and said, "Did you hear what that Canadian Bishop said? The Canadian Bishops were suggesting the ordination of married men!" I just grinned at him and chuckled a little. All of a sudden I saw the shock on his face. "My God!" he said, "You are the one who made the intervention!"

I informed him that the Canadian Bishops, by majority, were still in favour of celibacy as the general rule. We were not suggesting a wholesale abandonment of the charism of celibacy. We were simply trying to come to grips with some particularly difficult situations. I told him we had in mind Latin America, where sometimes there was only a handful of Native priests and where there were many complex social situations. I stressed that fidelity in marriage seemed to be a more necessary sign in some areas than celibacy, since I knew firsthand that in the missions where my own priests were serving, even though there were many baptisms, the baptism of the child of a married couple was the exception. Most of the couples were not legally married.

Some of the Bishops were very much in agreement with us. As a matter of fact, the Bishop of Mira came to me afterwards and told me that he had been afraid to make an intervention but that I had now given him the courage to do so. The next day he gave a very strong intervention in which he said that the days of the white missionary were finished. His Order had men working with the Natives along the valleys of the rivers in Africa. The Bishop went on to state that soon white missionaries would not be able to continue to function in that particular part of the world. In fact, he thought he would probably be the last of the missionary Bishops there. "Who is going to take our place?" he asked. "They will not want white missionaries. If we do not have permission to prepare some of the Native married men for ordination to the priesthood in order to continue our work," he said, "then I am afraid that the faith is liable to die out there."

Cardinal Suenens brought up a similar argument on this whole question. He suggested that, at some time, in some circumstances, we were going to have to choose between the Eucharist and the charism of celibacy. He asked which was more important and where would justice lie if the people were deprived of the Eucharist simply because of an ecclesiastical disciplinary law.

This remains a very serious question today when there are sometimes two or three of our parishes being served by only one priest and the number of priests continues to diminish. At the same time, we witness the dedicated and devoted service of married clergy in our sister Christian Churches. After all these years, I still find it difficult to understand the attitude of the authorities of the Church towards the possibility of ordaining married men. I do not think that the Sacrament of Marriage is an impediment *per se*. Why would one Sacrament impede the reception of another?

Memoirs

The long tradition of celibacy of the clergy has been one of the good things in our Church, but perhaps it is time that this question be faced more honestly and more openly in view of the conditions in which we live today. Surely we should be humble enough to pray, to think, to debate, to exchange views on a subject of such vital importance and such immediacy for the future of the Church. With prayerful reflection and honest exchange of opinions we might come to the point where we find not just *an* answer but the *right* answer.

On the occasion of the twentieth anniversary of the 1971 Synod, Tom Harpur, a Toronto author and broadcaster, wrote a very interesting article and with his permission I quote it here in its entirety.

Toronto Star, Sunday, October 6, 1991

Celibacy still dogs Rome 20 years after heroic speech

Exactly 20 years ago I was in Rome covering my first foreign assignment as religion editor of The Star. The occasion was a 30-day synod of bishops from around the world to deal with the nature, purpose and shape of the priesthood in today's society.

I remember it all vividly for a number of reasons but particularly because of the furor and excitement caused by the Canadian delegation to the meetings. They quick-

ly became the delight of the international media corps because of their progressive views and their willingness to be quite informal and frank with reporters. Given the general air of obfuscation and reserve that otherwise surrounded events at the Vatican that fall, they stood out like heroes.

What kicked it all off, though, was the famous speech of Most Rev. Alexander Carter (now retired), who was bishop of Sault Ste. Marie and president of the Canadian Bishops' Conference at the time. Carter, the brother of G. Emmett Cardinal Carter, former Archbishop of Toronto, rose in the synod on Oct. 9, 1971 to make an eloquent plea on behalf of Canadian bishops and priests for a new look at the issue of compulsory celibacy. He called for the ordination of married men to the priesthood.

Because this is the 20th anniversary of that speech, or "intervention" as it is called technically, and since the climate in the Roman Catholic Church today is so much more restrictive than it was then - only six years after the close of Vatican II - it is useful to be reminded of what Carter actually dared to say on behalf of Canadian Catholics.

Carter led off by noting that, while celibacy was not really on the agenda of the synod, it was impossible to avoid it. "It is an issue which has to be faced honestly and frankly, and which can hardly be termed peripheral," he told the assembly. He took exception to the fact that the document produced by the Curia to introduce the synod's topic showed "an unhealthy obsession with celibacy" to the point where there was a real risk of "erod-

ing the very nature of the priesthood rather than admit married men to Holy Orders."

He pointed out, rightly, that nobody was questioning the fact that celibacy has great value where people have been given the "charism" or gift of living a celibate life. But, he added, "Our research shows that many of our priests are living celibate lives for motives which are considerably inferior to those traditionally advanced by the Church." Where being celibate was an act of compulsion rather than of free choice - "ultimate freedom" - it easily becomes not a blessing but a stumbling-block, he said.

In asking for a change in the discipline, Carter stressed he and his fellow clergy were not suggesting getting rid of celibacy altogether: "the charism will always remain."

With this as preamble, he then dropped the thunderbolt: "Canadian bishops are nearly unanimous in favor of ordaining mature married men where there is need, and also a small majority are in favor of changing the present discipline to provide for the ordination of married men independently of need. And 90 per cent of our priests are of the same mind."

The bishop explained the call for married priests as coming from the conviction that married men "who have the experience of family life, and of life in the heart of the secular world, have a new and valuable dimension to bring to the priesthood." He described the current practice of restricting candidates for priesthood largely to young men who have spent all of their adult life in schools, colleges and seminaries and said "our world and our churches now may need other types too."

Carter said the bishops would like to see priests who have been properly dispensed and are now married (there are at least 110,000 of these worldwide) readmitted to the exercise of their priesthood but that it would not be feasible "until our people learn to see that married men can be priests and ... realize there is not an essential connection between celibacy and priesthood."

In a view that sharply contrasts with some of the speeches pro obligatory celibacy by the present Pope, Carter said many priests are not opposed to celibacy "for selfish reasons" but because they believe optional celibacy would be a more effective witness, especially to young people, in a society "where the passionate desire for freedom has taken on a new dimension."

The most moving part of his speech came at the end where Carter said part of the concern to see a change in the law of celibacy flowed from "the suffering, even agony, of some bishops and many priests in the face of the present discipline regarding celibacy."

If anything, this clerical suffering and agony has increased in the intervening two decades. What's more the number of Catholic parishes worldwide with no priest at all now stands at 50 per cent. This means that millions of ordinary Catholics now must endure the suffering and spiritual loss of having no regular sacramental life whatever.

Memoirs

Currently the bishops everywhere have been told not even to dialogue with married priests. They are not free to differ openly on mandatory celibacy as Carter once did. The ordination of women, also mooted later by the Canadian bishops, can't even be mentioned in today's Catholic Church.

It's 20 years later, but the Church, alas, is no further ahead.

Following the discussion on the Priesthood, the 1971 Synod went on to address the problem of the Third World and Social Justice. There is no doubt that this Synod had a significant role to play in helping the Church to start a new campaign for justice since it was clearly stated that Social Justice is a constitutive part of evangelization. It was also one of the first times, in a large international event of this nature, that the transnational and multinational corporations were being called into question. As a matter of fact, it was so important that it brought many of the leading journalists from around the world to our doorstep. The French newspaper, *Le Monde*, was particularly interested.

Father William Ryan, S.J., a professional economist and our consultant on Social Justice, had come over to Rome with Cardinal Flahiff and myself. We wanted him at the Synod for this topic in particular because he was very much involved and well informed on matters of Social Justice.

Earlier on I had accompanied Father Ryan to Washington, D.C. as Vice-Chairman of the

Alex Carter

Committee responsible for promoting the Centre of Concern, which Ryan had been asked to establish. This Centre was to be supported by the American Jesuits and the American Bishops. It was to pursue the whole question of Social Justice in today's world, to establish principles based upon recent Papal Encyclicals and to educate the people on the obligations that Social Justice imposes, particularly at the international level.

On behalf of the Canadian Bishops, I had the task of making an intervention in which I questioned the power and the accountability of multinational corporations. I also referred to the billions of dollars being used for armaments by the United States. I gave a picture of ourselves too, as Canadian neighbours, sitting next to the United States with their vast amount of power. I used Prime Minister Trudeau's simile - and I said it was Trudeau's - about the mouse and the elephant. It received quite a reaction!

At coffee break Archbishop Rembert Weakland of Milwaukee, who was then Dom Rembert Weakland, Abbot Primate of the International Benedictine Confederation, came to me and said, "Alex, that was quite a comparison between the United States and Canada - the elephant and the mouse. I think it was perfectly right about the elephant, but I do not think it was exactly right about the mouse. It may have been more exact to have said a porcupine!"

Following my intervention, two others were made on behalf of the Canadian Bishops.

Memoirs

Archbishop Plourde of Ottawa made an excellent intervention on the nature of justice. Cardinal Flahiff of Winnipeg, in his intervention, included the suggestion that the role of women in the Church would have to be studied in the interest of justice. He also proposed that an International Commission be named by the Holy Father to study this issue.

As an aside, I remember leaving the hall and chatting outside with Cardinal Flahiff. We met Barbara Ward, a leader in the struggle for Social Justice in the United States. She had given a magnificent talk on the subject at the beginning of the Synod. Of course, Barbara Ward, on that subject, was always moving and exciting. When she saw us there she planted a big kiss on each of us and said, "I love the Canadian Bishops!"

When the Synod later published Cardinal Flahiff's intervention, there was an interesting by-play because part of his report had been tampered with. Apparently a meeting had been called by some of the members of the Synod Social Justice Committee and the reference to women was extracted. Fortunately this was spotted and brought up at the general meeting the next day. The Bishops wanted to know who was responsible, who had called the committee meeting and why this text, on which we had already voted, was changed. Cardinal John J. Wright, the Prefect of the Congregation for the Clergy, was in the chair.

He said, "Obviously the man who can answer this question is Cardinal Tarrancon since he is the

President of that committee. Would the Cardinal like to tell us about the meeting?"

Tarrancon answered, "I know of no meeting. I was not invited to any meeting. I was not present at any meeting. I do not know who called it or why they called it and I do not know who authorized a change in the text."

There was an uncomfortable moment in the hall after that particular development. I would also like to mention in passing that I find it rather amusing that, although the Bishops of the Synod had accepted almost unanimously the proposal for an International Commission to study the role of women, it took two and a half years before any action was taken. It was only about six months before the next Synod was to convene that a Commission was finally organized and named. Had nothing been done, it would have been extremely difficult to explain why a decision made by the preceding Synod on the role of women had been ignored.

***

During that 1971 Synod I was inadvertently thrust into a position of more publicity than I had expected. It so happened that the priest who was supposed to be the representative from the Synod to the English-speaking press took sick and, at the last minute, could not make it. They pressed a Dutchman into service but his English was so heavily accented that the English and American press had difficulty in understanding him. One or two from the international press group learned that some of the Canadian Bishops were staying at the Christopher Columbus hotel, around the corner from the Vatican. They started coming to the hotel and Archbishop Plourde and I very often found ourselves surrounded by eight or ten correspondents from various countries. They would sit and chat with us and we would discuss what was occurring at the Synod. They seemed to appreciate the fact that they were getting firsthand information.

The English and American international press group invited me to speak at their monthly dinner meeting which was being held at a Trattoria across the Tiber. They had taken the restaurant over for that night. The meeting attracted many correspondents who packed the room to hear my talk on what was happening at the Synod and to be present for the question and answer period that was to follow. As a matter of fact, the President, who was an American and a very charming gentleman, told me it was the largest crowd they had had since Elizabeth Taylor and Richard Burton had attended one of their meetings!

***

As I mentioned earlier, I made an intervention at the Synod on multinational corporations and on their accountability, particularly because of the immense amounts of money they had as compared to most of the poorer nations of the world. I received a message shortly afterwards from the United Nations Centre in Geneva. There was to be a meeting in Mexico dealing precisely with the question of Social Justice in the developing nations. I was invited to Geneva to meet the people who were to attend the meeting in Mexico and to go with them as a participant. I wired back immediately, saying that I personally was not qualified to accept such an assignment because I had merely presented a paper based upon the discussions of our theologians and Bishops together. I advised them that Father William Ryan, S.J., the chief architect of this particular paper, was with me in Rome and that he would be far more valuable to them than I would. I felt that Father Ryan was much more knowledgeable and that he would be better able to render this service.

Bill Ryan later went to Mexico upon the invitation of the Commission for Development in the Third World. I mention this simply to record the fact that the thinking of the Canadian Bishops at that time was certainly very well received by representatives from the various countries at the Synod. As a matter of fact, I had been asked by most of the Bishops who were at the Synod from Africa and India for a copy of our intervention the very day I gave it. It was evident that the Canadian Bishops were, at that point - and it is to our credit - right on target.

***

Sometime before the Synod, I was interviewed by the editor of *America*, the Jesuit publication in

Memoirs

New York, and that interview was published by them. It dealt with *Humanae Vitae*, priestly celibacy, and other such issues. During the Synod, the Papal Delegate to Canada came to see me. He said he had received a letter from the Secretary of State and that the Holy Father was a little offended by whatever I had said in the article - in fact, he seemed to read some implied or suggested criticism in my commentary. So I said to the Papal Delegate, "What do you want me to do?"

He suggested that while I was in Rome I should speak with the Pope, and he offered to set up an appointment for me.

The appointment was scheduled for eleven o'clock in the morning, so I went over to the Vatican about half an hour early. I chatted with the Pope's Secretary who said to me, "This place is in an uproar! Your appointment is for eleven but at eleven-thirty the Pope is receiving, for the first time, the President of the Soviet Union. We were told at the last moment by the Soviet Ambassador that, wherever the President goes or whenever he receives anyone for an audience, he smokes a cigar. That is very important to him, and he wants the right to smoke a cigar when he is having his audience with the Pope."

You can imagine the confusion in the Vatican. I do not suppose that anyone has ever smoked in the presence of the Holy Father, and certainly not during the last few centuries. But as a courtesy, some of the Vatican staff were running around Rome trying to find the best cigars for the President!

When I went in to see Pope Paul, he greeted me very cordially. I told him I was sorry that there seemed to have been some misunderstanding concerning my article. I said that I hoped we could clear the matter up quickly since I understood that he was receiving the President of the Soviet Union after I left, and I was sure he would like a few free moments before such an important audience.

Pope Paul turned to me and said, "Bishop Carter, your appointment is for half an hour and we will spend that half hour talking together."

With that we sat down and chatted. Any difficulties that had arisen as a result of my article in *America* were resolved. Our conversation became very friendly and I left with a warm send-off and a number of beautiful rosaries bearing his coat of arms. I have always kept the fondest memories of that man. He was so kind and so gentle.

***

In that year of 1971, I also took on the task of Canadian Director for the Propagation of the Faith in the English sector, where I served for six years. Bishop Gilles Ouellet, then Bishop of Gaspé, was Director in the French sector. The two of us served slightly longer terms, perhaps because they did not want to change National Directors at a time when

Memoirs

new rules were being made for the Propagation of the Faith throughout the world. We had been debating some issues for several years and there had been, as usual, a difference of opinion between the central authorities of the Congregation and the National Directors. For example, we tried to find ways and means of giving the National Directors more freedom to organize their campaigns in the way they thought best, according to the circumstances in their own countries.

Bishop Ouellet and I were chosen to represent the Canadian Bishops at the Pontifical Missionary Council, and we went to Rome together. Towards the end of our stay there, a new Constitution was being drawn up. He and I became very interested in it and we argued a great deal in favour of decentralization.

Of course, there has always been a tendency in Rome to centralize everything so we were not surprised to find that they wanted to dot every "i" and cross every "t". They wanted to ensure that there would be no loophole that would allow a National Director to take any action without authorization from the central body. In spite of that, I think we made a certain contribution. Both Gilles and I intervened a few times. We became, in a way, the spokesmen for some of the missionary Bishops who would ask us to bring up issues for them because they were afraid to do so themselves. These Bishops depended so much upon the revenue that came from the Congregation for the Propagation of the Faith that they obviously did not want to antagonize the General Secretary of the Congregation or the Cardinal Prefect or anyone else in authority. As a result, we were probably a cause of annoyance to some members of the Congregation.

It is rather ironical and amusing that when our term was over the Congregation notified the Bishops that they no longer wanted a residential Bishop appointed as Director of the Propagation of the Faith. They had no objection to an Auxiliary Bishop. Since Gilles and I were probably the only two residential Bishops serving the Congregation at the time, I think this was more "ad personam" than "ad rem". I suspect that ruling was made with us in mind.

Actually neither one of us was going to let our name stand anyway. We had done our share - in fact, more than our share - because our term had been prolonged. We both had felt the pressure of the work in our own dioceses. The demands had been great because we were serious about implementing the teachings of the Council and, in my case, carrying out the recommendations of our diocesan 'Little Council'. With full programs underway in our own dioceses, we were both very happy to hand this responsibility over to someone else.

***

Apart from my term as National Director for the Propagation of the Faith from 1971 to 1977 and my service as a member of the Secretariat for Non-Believers from 1967 to 1973, the Synod of 1971 was the last time I was to play a major role as a representative of the Canadian Bishops in Rome. My participation in the CCCB from then on was simply that of a member. Aside from the general meetings, most of my service was given to the Social Affairs Commission and later to the Laity Commission.

The Social Affairs Commission opened up a whole new possibility for the Bishops to bring their contribution on justice and sharing to the people of our country and to the people of the Third World. The Laity Commission, to my way of thinking, never fully realized its objective in the CCCB. This was not necessarily through anyone's fault. The subject is so vast and there are so many ways of interpreting how the role of the lay people can best be incorporated into our Church that it was really a difficult task. I must say that the Bishops, both French-speaking and English-speaking, who served with me on that Commission were, from the very beginning, devoted to the ideal. They were convinced of the Church's need to have meaningful representation of our lay people. We needed people who would bring to the Bishops a greater and deeper realization of the increasing concerns of the laity in this day and age.

I have to say that, in general, I enjoyed the meetings of the CCCB. Our coming together was more than just work. It gave us an opportunity to know one another better, and in some cases, to become close friends. One incident in our fellowship that I remember is typical of the kind of relaxed relationship that we had.

As was the custom during our annual Plenary Assembly of the CCCB, the Apostolic Delegate held a reception for the Bishops. My brother Emmett and I attended, along with Archbishop Philip Pocock, Bishop Norman Gallagher, who was then Auxiliary Bishop in Montreal, and Bishop William Power of Antigonish. After the reception we had a slight delay. As we were leaving, the Apostolic Delegate asked Bishop Gallagher to wait a few minutes because he wanted to discuss something with him. The rest of us waited in the car. Knowing that there were one or two dioceses vacant and awaiting the appointment of a new Bishop, we decided to question Bishop Gallagher about this private conversation. When he arrived we pestered him, trying to find out what the Delegate had to say.

After many teasing questions about which diocese he would be going to, Gallagher said, "Well, I was not going to tell you, but since you insist - as I was leaving, the Apostolic Delegate pulled me aside and began asking me about Bishop Carter. I asked the Delegate 'Which one?' He answered, 'The nice one,' and I said to him, 'Oh, I didn't know there were three!'"

With that we all exploded with laughter and no further questions were asked of our quick-witted friend.

Audience with Pope John XXIII, 1962.

Carter with Pope Paul VI at the Synod in 1971.

Carter meets with the Archbishop of Canterbury, Michael Ramsey, 1969.

The Native people of the Diocese bestow the title of "honorary chief" on Carter.

Carter with Bishop Adolphe Proulx.

Surrounded by children in one of his many visits to the schools.

A visit to the Third World diocesan mission in Guatemala.

Carter's last official "Ad Limina" visit with Pope John Paul II. Bernard Pappin, Auxiliary Bishop accompanies him.

"The Bishop Alexander Carter Charitable Fund" is established in 1983. Carter is flanked by Ted Szilva, Dan Newell and Francis Donnelly, the founding board members.

Native people show gratitude in a Naming Ceremony, May 6, 1984. The name "Beedahbun" meaning "First Light of Dawn" is bestowed upon him.

A painting by Native artist Leland Bell entitled "Beedahbun" is presented to Carter by the University of Sudbury in recognition of his contribution as Chancellor.

With his niece Michele Carter and Bishop Bernard Pappin at the Pope's visit to the Martyrs Shrine in Midland, Ontario 1984.

Carter is officially invested as an Officer of the Order of Canada at Rideau Hall, Ottawa, by Governor General Jeanne Sauvé on October 18, 1989.

Living the Vision

*I*n the years following the Council I was able to devote much more attention to the hopes and needs of my own Diocese. I must say that those years remain a joy for me as I look back upon them. The Diocese of Sault Ste. Marie had long since become my home. There was, and there still is, a warmth about Northern Ontario and Catholic life here which you do not find everywhere. I do not know what it is about this Diocese, but I think I fell in love with the North after just a few years. I was happy to be able to spend more and more time with my priests and people, whom I had grown to love so much. My desire was to work with them to establish a local Church, as we had envisioned it in Vatican Council II. Together we began to realize the possibilities for the future of our Church.

The Diocese of Sault Ste. Marie is so widespread that it soon became evident that some structural changes were necessary. I decided to address the geographical problem by formally dividing the

Diocese into three regions: North Bay, Sudbury and Sault Ste. Marie. Because of the existence of the two main language groups in the Diocese, we also officially acknowledged two sectors at that time. This may sound very complex but it makes sense if you consider the geography of the Diocese and the fact that there are two communities worshipping in completely different languages with practically equal numbers in both groups. There is no reason at all why there cannot be more than one community in a local Church. As a matter of fact, it has proven to work quite well in our own Diocese, where a third community, our Native people, would also be recognized as a sector.

I had been identifying and strengthening the French sector of the Diocese particularly with the aid of my French-speaking Auxiliary, but not without some difficulty. Having earlier sacrificed Adolphe Proulx to Alexandria, I later lost my second valued Auxiliary, Bishop Roger Despatie, when he was appointed to the Diocese of Hearst in 1973. That Diocese received a great Christian gentleman and a very good and holy Bishop, who served with dedication and devotion until his untimely death in 1993, after a long struggle with cancer. Roger had been a loyal assistant during his years in the Diocese and his leaving was a great loss.

Afterwards, I was fortunate enough to have another good man to serve as Episcopal Vicar to the French-speaking members of the Diocese, in the person of Monseigneur Eugène Lacourcière, the pastor of Sacré Coeur parish in Sturgeon Falls. He served during the two years that intervened between the departure of Bishop Despatie and the arrival of my new French-speaking Auxiliary, Bishop Gérard Dionne.

I had known Bishop Dionne from years before, when he was asked to come to the CCCB to serve on the Latin American Commission. I knew how well he had performed that task and fulfilled the role that he had been given. When the time came to replace Bishop Despatie, I was considering a few of my own men, but certainly my thoughts centered upon Gérard Dionne as a possible and desirable Auxiliary. I was particularly anxious to have someone of his background and calibre because the French sector was continuing to develop. The French Ministries Program had begun by this time. We had also decided that it was time to establish a Centre for the Franco-Ontarians and have offices where their various organizations and services could come together. In the meantime we were using the basement rooms of a parish for that purpose.

Happily, Bishop Dionne accepted to come. In the years that he was with us, he was certainly a tremendous help to me and to all of the Franco-Ontarians. The work that was begun by Bishop Proulx and continued and developed by Bishop Despatie came to full growth during the years that Bishop Dionne was with us, until he left to become Bishop of Edmunston early in 1984. Because of this man's organizational ability, his friendliness, his simplicity, and at the same time, his great wit and knowledge and his fine ability to bring out the best in people, they were rich years.

At the time of the appointment of Bishop Dionne, I had also asked for and received an Auxiliary Bishop for the English sector of the Diocese. Bishop Bernard Pappin was with me for the rest of my years as Bishop and I cannot say enough about his loyalty and his generosity. He was always willing to undertake anything he was asked to do. He shared my vision of the role of the laity in our local Church. He was a good person to have at Diocesan and Regional Pastoral Council meetings. I left to him a great deal of the carrying out of the policies and decisions arrived at by the Bishop and the people serving on the various committees. The close friendship we have shared throughout these many years continues to be a blessing in my life.

***

It was with the help of Father Don Ordendorff and Father Chester Warenda that we responded to the call of the Council for the restoration of the permanent diaconate. We founded a school for ministries in our Diocese in the early seventies, and I feel a great sense of gratitude for the work that these men did. They were inspired by their love for the laity and convinced of the role to be played by the laity in the life of the Church. Without them we would not have had a Ministries Program of such quality.

Memoirs

I think the most important aspect of our Ministries Program was the development of the whole family spirit. We had learned from others who had moved more quickly into the restoration of the permanent diaconate, that very often problems arose in the homes of the deacons after ordination. When these men had completed their training and had begun to perform various Offices in the Church under the direction of the parish priests, it sometimes brought difficulties into the family. When a wife did not quite understand what the Program and the Ministry entailed, it seemed to her that her husband was just too busy doing "his own thing". The deacons were too often absent from the home and from the normal sharing of life that goes on in a good family. In order to avoid this, we insisted that their wives and younger children take part in the monthly weekend sessions of the Program. They would accompany the men to the town of Espanola where, because it is geographically the central point in our large Diocese, we had established our school. I believe it was a wise decision. Having participated in the program, the wives, and to a certain extent the children, understood what the permanent diaconate and ministry in the Church was all about.

Not long after the Program began, at the request of the women, I agreed that they could actively participate in the studies if they chose to do so. Furthermore, I decided to form a womens' group in the Diocese, called the Diocesan Order of Women, which would be a kind of diaconate without ordination. The women who completed the Program were prepared to lead groups, to give talks and to participate in the religious education and spiritual development of parishioners' and groups within the parishes. They were trained during the Ministries Program to conduct paraliturgical ceremonies and to do works that Church law would not prohibit them from doing. At least we were beginning, at that time, to recognize that there was a new and more vital role for women in the Church. This role is still far from having been clearly thought out and should be receiving in-depth study in the Church. As early as 1970 this issue was a matter of concern to me and I still feel very strongly about it.

That year, I remember receiving a letter from a woman in Toronto asking my opinion about the possibility of the restoration of the diaconate for women. In fact, she suggested that, if she could find enough women who, like herself, felt a compelling need to assist in the spiritual ministry of the Church, it would then seem appropriate to present a petition to the Bishops of Canada requesting their consideration of this matter. She indicated that she was aware of the strong reaction among what she called "old-fashioned Catholics" against the ordination of women to the priesthood, but with Early Christian precedent for the diaconate, there might be fewer objections. She felt that younger Catholics were slipping away from the Church because the Church was failing to act in this and other delicate areas, and that such a move might give hope to them and to women who had so much to contribute

Memoirs

to the life of the Church. Because this committed Christian woman was convinced that all were called to hear Christ's command to "make disciples of all nations", her question was this: Did I think that deaconesses would fill a need and stand some chance of being accepted in the Church?

This was my reply:

I read your letter with much interest. Personally I would be in favour of re-establishing the office of deaconess in the Church.

It is hard to say why the diaconate should be renewed without taking into consideration the vast possibilities that are offered to the Church in the number of women willing, anxious and able to participate in sacramental form in the renewal of the Church. I think that participation of women in the restoration of the diaconate would also bear out the wish of the Council that women take their proper place in the Church as first class members and with full equality. The question of the priesthood at the moment is still far too contentious. We may have to leave consideration of that for a later date. But I think the time is now ripe for women to receive an official and sacramental mandate from the Church.

Therefore I encourage you to carry out your intention in gathering a few interested and knowledgeable women to present a petition to the Canadian Bishops. Such a move would initiate discussion among the Bishops and this is the first necessary step in any change of legislation.

Alex Carter

Thank you for writing me. Be assured of my interest in this whole matter.

With all good wishes, I am

> *Yours sincerely in Our Lord,*
> *Alexander Carter*
> *Bishop of Sault Ste. Marie*

Our Ministries Program initially caused some strong reaction from many of my brother Bishops and even more so when I extended an almost equivalent role to the women in our Diocese, as I have just mentioned. I was challenged quite volubly and forcefully at a few of the meetings of the Canadian Bishops which I attended afterwards. Some of the Bishops were asking me what I was trying to do. It seemed to them unthinkable that I would be mandating women for ministry in the Church. In response I simply told them that I thought the time was right and that they might be doing it themselves some day.

A few years later, we had that memorable meeting of the CCCB to which we had invited women representatives from across the country. We listened to their request for recognition of the role that women should be playing in the Church. At the dinner after the meeting, I was seated at table with four or five Bishops who began asking me, "How did you go about bringing women into Ministry in your Diocese?" It seemed that those Bishops who had been most vocal in their criticism a few years earlier were now interested in knowing how we went about it! I tell this story because it shows how things move in our Church and how some of our positions change as time goes on.

***

I felt that these were the years in which some of our hopes were beginning to be realized in the Diocese. We had begun to live the basic, fundamental message of the Council, and our Church was becoming more than just an organization of people believing in God and professing the Catholic faith. It was becoming a communion in which there was more sharing. We listened to each other more and there was more acceptance of one another. Life was more peaceful in our parishes, among our clergy and in our organizations. Though the field of education remained a place where there was misunderstanding, competition and friction between groups, even there the situation had become a little less contentious and more reasonable than it had been for too many years.

***

A long-standing problem in our Diocese was the need to provide funding for the Catholic High Schools which were owned and operated by Religious Congregations. This challenge precipitated the establishment of the Pot 'O' Gold Lottery.

Some of the Religious Communities had indicated that they could no longer provide full financial support for their schools and the very existence of Catholic Secondary Education was threatened. In response, a group of concerned citizens in Sudbury had inaugurated a financial campaign to assist in the short-term, by providing funding for a period of three years.

It was during this time that a small delegation from the Executive of this campaign came to see me. After looking at all the alternatives they felt that a long-term solution was necessary. Their proposal was a provincial lottery.

It should come as no surprise that I had many reservations. I expected that adverse comments and publicity might be generated if a lottery were operated under the auspices of the Diocese of Sault Ste. Marie. I did make a proposal to the Ontario Conference of Catholic Bishops suggesting that they consider operating a lottery for the benefit of Catholic education throughout the entire province. The Conference rejected the idea.

Because our situation was so desperate, it began to appear to me that holding a lottery presented the only possible solution to our problem. I told everyone concerned that if a better solution was presented, I would gladly accept it. None was forthcoming, so after much prayer and discernment I decided to let the initial delegation proceed in attempting to secure a provincial lottery license. The

Memoirs

proceeds from the proposed lottery would provide the financial assistance necessary for the funding of Catholic High Schools in our Diocese and would also help support charitable organizations throughout Northern Ontario.

I did not want to leave any stone unturned in assuring the continuation of Catholic education for our young people, particularly after so many years of struggle. I knew it was not the lottery, but the possible abuse of it, that could be criticized.

After much consultation with the Ontario government and in particular with the Lotteries Commissioner, we were granted a license to operate a lottery throughout most of Ontario. The Pot 'O' Gold Lottery was launched in the fall of 1980 and the first draw was held on January 1, 1981.

To ensure that we were above suspicion in all our dealings, we put into place the best possible system of accountability. I appointed a group of well-respected business people to the Board of Directors for Northern Charities, Diocese of Sault Ste. Marie Inc., the company formed to operate the Pot 'O' Gold Lottery. The head office was in Sudbury. I insisted that the Board appoint a reputable auditing firm to oversee the entire operation.

The lottery ran for four years and was most successful. With a staff of only two people, Sudbury businessmen Ted Szilva and Dan Newell managed the day-to-day operations and guided its direction until 1984, when full funding for Ontario's Catholic Secondary Schools became a reality. During those four years of operation, millions of dollars were given to Catholic education in Northern Ontario. Charitable organizations such as Native Peoples' projects, homes for the mentally challenged, alcohol and drug addiction centres and half-way houses, to name only a few, also received financial asistance from the lottery proceeds.

In 1983, knowing that the lottery was soon to be discontinued, the Board of Directors of the Pot 'O' Gold Lottery established a permanent fund called the Bishop Alexander Carter Charitable Fund. This would ensure on-going financial support for the many needy charitable organizations that were providing necessary services here in the North. A new Board of Directors was appointed to administer the Fund. Ted Szilva, Dan Newell, Francis Donnelly (a prominent Sudbury lawyer) and myself filled the positions on that Board and it was decided that, upon my retirement as Bishop, the new Bishop of this Diocese would join us on the Board.

The profits earned from the Lottery had been sizeable and they were invested, providing the Carter Fund with a healthy interest with which to support many worthy charities. To date, almost one million dollars has been distributed annually.

***

As the years went by our appreciation of the Native People in our Diocese grew and their rights

Memoirs

became more and more recognized. An agreement was reached between the Diocese and the English-speaking Jesuit Fathers to establish the Anishinabe Spiritual Centre at Anderson Lake, near Espanola, in the heart of the Native communities and Reserves of our Diocese. The Jesuits agreed to supply priests to operate the Centre, and it was to be jointly financed by the Jesuits and the Diocese. The Anishinabe Spiritual Centre became an important element in the life of the Native community. We had already initiated a Native Peoples' Ministry Program, and there were many Native Deacons serving in their own communities. This Program was moved to the new Centre and widened in scope.

The Native Peoples were seeing new leadership arising from within their own ranks. We saw the emergence of people who were becoming charismatic leaders. We encouraged the Native People to rediscover their roots and to value their own culture and the beauties of some of their own ceremonies and early traditions. We tried to bring our Liturgy into relationship with the culture and the yearnings of our Native People. Some of the older Jesuit missionaries, I think, were a little critical of our approach and not always convinced that we were on the right track. However, I am certain that, as with many things, the good that was being done overshadowed any misunderstanding or any slight exaggerations that might have crept in during that process.

Our Native People have truly become an essential part of the life of our local Church and I think that Bishop Gervais, my successor, was quite right in recognizing three sectors in the Diocese - not just the French-speaking and English-speaking sectors, but also the Native People's sector.

I would like to reiterate that I have expressed very clearly my own personal conviction that we should be ordaining married Native men as priests. I have not changed my mind in my retirement. It does not concern me officially now, since I no longer have the responsibility for the Church of Sault Ste. Marie. However, even in my retirement, without trying to break any rules or regulations, I am still convinced - even more convinced than ever - that we are very short-sighted in not giving the Native People their own Native married priests.

As I mentioned before, having had three parishes in Guatemala, I realized that there, too, the local Bishops should have the right to make a decision on whether or not they need some married Guatemalan men as priests. Just to stand back and say "Never!", and refuse to discuss the issue, is not a solution.

Again I say this without casting any doubt as to the importance of celibacy in the clergy. It is still desirable as a charism. But there are situations where, because of the rule of celibacy, we could be depriving our people of something to which they have a right.

***

Memoirs

During my years as Bishop of Sault Ste. Marie, the Ontario Bishops formed the Ontario Conference of Catholic Bishops. The OCCB has grown into a very useful instrument and has the great advantage of bringing the Bishops together on a regular basis. The fellowship that we shared while addressing the various problems which arose in Ontario, helped each of us in our own dioceses and encouraged us, as a group, to form a greater unity in this, the most populous province of Canada. It also provided us with the opportunity to meet with the Premier of Ontario and other political leaders of the Province once or twice a year. There were so many things happening in Ontario that it was a blessing that we were able to get together and share our thoughts and feelings as we did. There was always a very warm spirit in this group. Not only did we work together, share together and pray together - but we also had good times together. We had our moments of serious fraternal exchange and our moments of enjoyable and pleasurable fellowship.

When I was President of the Ontario Bishops during the time of the consultation on the Canadian Constitution in Ottawa, delegations were being sent to speak on the "Right to Life" and particularly on the matter of abortion. At the CCCB we had a lawyer help us draw up a statement on behalf of the Canadian Bishops concerning abortion. It was to be presented to the Parliamentary Committee responsible for the changes in the Constitution. Just a few days before Christmas, I received a call from the General Secretary of the CCCB, Monsignor Dennis

Murphy. He asked me if the Ontario Bishops would consent to appear before the Committee because the CCCB could not get an agreement from their Executive to send representatives on their behalf. I did not think that we could replace the CCCB, but I agreed that if no one from there would make the presentation, then I would accept to go as President of the Ontario Bishops and present the paper that the CCCB had drawn up. They gave me the information, and I went to Ottawa to represent the Ontario Bishops. I had asked Archbishop Plourde, Vice-President of the OCCB, to accompany me. We presented our paper and answered questions. We had been allotted twenty minutes to a half-hour but we were there for almost an hour. I think it was a worthwhile hearing and exchange.

This debate over the question of representation from the Canadian Bishops underlines the fact that Canada is not an easy place for united action by the Church. I think it is something that occasionally hinders our pastoral efforts. It is also a reminder that we have a great deal of difference in our approach to issues in the various regions of our country. The above example alone gives us much food for reflection and shows the need for much prayer. It definitely weakened the Catholic point of view by having Ontario Bishops speak for themselves because they could not speak on behalf of all the Bishops of Canada.

***

Memoirs

The last years of my ministry as Bishop passed very quickly. When I reached the age of seventy-five, not only did I feel obliged to accept the new regulation following Vatican II that a bishop offer his resignation at that age, but I was actually very anxious to have it acted upon quickly. Two letters - one to the Nuncio, followed a couple of months later by one to the Pope - stipulated that I felt a change should take place as quickly as possible. I explained that a Diocese as important and as large as ours needed a man in the fullness of his life and health if the job was to be done as it should. Finally my request was granted and it was with a very special joy that I learned that I would be succeeded by Bishop Marcel Gervais, whom I had admired so much in the years since his ordination. His work in London, his presence in so many organizations of the Church and his great Scripture study series, *Journey*, were among his contributions to the people and to the Bishops of the Church. I had hoped that my successor would be a man of his calibre.

***

As I draw these reflections to their conclusion, I would like to say that they are special and important to me, mostly in the sense that, in preparing them, I have remembered the many people to whom I am indebted. I cannot name them all; nor can I even begin to express adequately the heavy debt of gratitude I feel for so many who are very dear to me. All I can do is assure them of my love, my affection, my happy memories and my prayers.

CHRONOLOGY

April 16, 1909	Alexander Carter was born in Montreal, Quebec, the son of Thomas Carter and Mary Kerr.
1915 - 1924	Primary education at St. Patrick's School, Montreal.
1924 - 1930	Secondary education at Collège de Montréal.
1930 - 1932	Attended Séminaire de Philosophie Received the degree of Bachelor of Arts.
1932 - 1936	Attended Grand Séminaire de Montréal. Received the degree of Licentiate in Sacred Theology (L.Th.), Université de Montréal.
June 6, 1936	Ordained a priest in St. James' Cathedral, Montreal, by Bishop Alphonse-Emmanuel Deschamps.
1936 - 1937	Curate at St. Anthony's Parish, Montreal.

1937 - 1939	Studied at the S. Appolinaris Institute in Rome. Received the degree of Licentiate in Canon Law. Resided at the Canadian College.
1939 - 1946	Vice-Chancellor of the Archdiocese of Montreal and Chaplain of St. Mary's Hospital.
1946 - 1947	Chancellor of the Archdiocese of Winnipeg, Manitoba.
1948 - 1954	Vice-Officialis of the Metropolitan Tribunal of the Archdiocese of Montreal and Chaplain of St. Mary's Hospital.
1955 - 1957	Pastor of Holy Family Parish, Montreal.
Dec. 10, 1956	Appointed Titular Bishop of Sita and Coadjutor Bishop of the Diocese of Sault Ste. Marie, Ontario.
Feb. 2, 1957	Consecrated Bishop in Notre Dame Basilica, Montreal, by His Eminence Paul-Emile Cardinal Léger.

Nov. 1957	Appointed Apostolic Administrator of the Diocese of Sault Ste. Marie, Ontario.
Nov. 22, 1958	Succeeds as Bishop of the Diocese of Sault Ste. Marie, Ontario.
1959 - 1985	Chancellor of the University of Sudbury.
Oct. 11, 1962 to Dec. 8, 1962	Attended the first session of the Second Vatican Council.
1962	Received an Honorary Doctorate, Laurentian University of Sudbury.
Sept. 29, 1963 to Dec. 4, 1963	Attended the second session of the Second Vatican Council.
Sept. 14, 1964 to Nov. 21, 1964	Attended the third session of the Second Vatican Council.
Sept. 14, 1965 to Dec. 8, 1965	Attended the final session of the Second Vatican Council.
1965 - 1967	Vice-President of the Canadian Conference of Catholic Bishops.
1967 - 1969	President of the Canadian Conference of Catholic Bishops.

Sept. 27, 1968	Canadian Bishops' statement on the encyclical *Humanae Vitae*.
1967 - 1973	Member of the Pontifical Council for Dialogue with Non-Believers.
1969, 1971	Delegate of the Canadian Bishops at two Synods in Rome.
Oct. 15, 1969	Intervention at the Synod of Bishops on the topic of Collegiality.
Oct. 8, 1971	Intervention at the Synod of Bishops on the topic of Priestly Celibacy.
1971 - 1977	National Director for Pontifical Mission Aid Societies for Canada.
1973 - 1977	Member of the Board of Governors of the Canadian Catholic Organization for Development and Peace.
1977 - 1981	President of the Ontario Conference of Catholic Bishops.
1978 - 1982	Chairman of the CCCB Episcopal Commission for the Laity.

1985	Resigned as Bishop of the Diocese of Sault Ste. Marie, Ontario.
Oct. 18, 1989	Officially invested as an Officer of the Order of Canada at Rideau Hall by Governor General Jeanne Sauvé.

924016